PORTRA
OF MY VICTOR

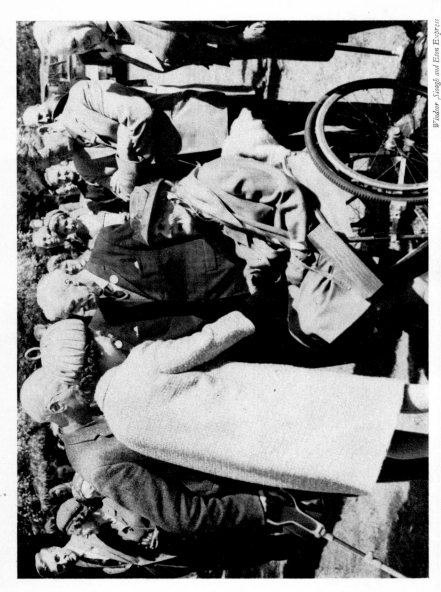

Meeting the Queen 1968

PORTRAIT OF MY VICTORIAN YOUTH

ALICE POLLOCK

JOHNSON

———

LONDON

First Published 1971
Reprinted 1971
ISBN 0 85307 097 0

Made and printed in Great Britain by Morrison & Gibb Ltd.,
London and Edinburgh

Johnson Publications Ltd., 11/14 Stanhope Mews West, London, S.W.7

CONTENTS

Introduction   by The Hon. Lady Farrer

CONTENTS

PART TWO

Natural and Supernatural

ILLUSTRATIONS

ACKNOWLEDGEMENTS

We should like to thank the *Windsor, Eton and Slough Express*
for permission to reproduce the Frontispiece, and also Colin
G. Futcher, A.I.I.P., of Haslemere, for his work on copies
of the old photographs, and for permission to reproduce
the original taken on the author's hundredth birthday.

INTRODUCTION

by

The Hon. Lady Farrer

The author of this book is now aged a hundred and two. When the Franco-Prussian War broke out she was two years old. She has lived through the South African War and two World Wars, in six reigns, under nineteen Prime Ministers and from man's first attempts to fly to two moon landings—a stretch of memories not often achieved.

The story of her youth during Victorian times makes a strange contrast to the conditions of youth today.

I first remember Alice Pollock fifty-six years ago when I was nineteen, just the age to appreciate two great qualities of hers—consideration for the opinions of the young and an unbiased and sympathetic understanding. But her greatest attraction to me and to everyone who knew her well was her sixth sense, her phenomenal power to see both into the past and the future. In her generation Alice's psychic powers were considered by those in a position to judge to be genuine and outstanding. Had she cared to, she could have become a successful medium, but she had always believed that this is a gift which cannot be used "on demand", and that to commercialise it is to debase it.

Her uncritical interest in other people is as keen as ever and I still enjoy a talk with her as much as I did all those years ago. It is common enough for the very old to retain clear recollections of bygone days, it is less usual for them to keep awareness of the world around them and re-membrance of the recent past as she has done.

Alice is the proud possessor of the two letters written by Nelson to Admiral the Honourable Sir William Cornwallis, the uncle of her grandmother, Lady Jemima Wykeham-Martin. The first of these letters, (which will be found in Appendix One), dated 1788, is written with Nelson's right hand, and the other is written five months before the Battle of Trafalgar with his left hand. Lady Jemima was the daughter of the 5th Earl Cornwallis; her second son, Alice's uncle, Fiennes, was one of the few survivors of the ill-fated "Charge of the Light Brigade". He wrote a letter (also to be found in the Appendix) to his stepmother describing the battle. Alice's mother was a sister of the 1st Lord Llangattock. Alice was, accordingly, first cousin of the Hon. C. S. Rolls, joint founder of Rolls-Royce.

To see her now you would not believe that she had reached such a great age. Despite increasing deafness and trouble with her eyes, her sense of humour is unfailing and I have never known her to make more than a passing reference to her disabilities.

In 1968 the meeting of The Royal Forestry Society was held at Reading and the first visit was to Windsor. The Queen announced her intention of being present informally. On the 6th May Alice was driven to Windsor Great Park, where a little later the Queen arrived. A few presentations were made, including two Foresters, who, after fifty years of working membership, were made honorary Life Members of the Society. The Queen shook hands with Alice and spoke of her hundred years. The reply was "This is my birthday treat, to have the honour of being presented to Your Majesty and I am enjoying every minute of it."

When the question of celebrating her hundredth birthday arose, Alice said that she did not wish to have a party, but would like short visits of a few people at a time spread out over several weeks so that she could enjoy them individually. She also asked that the family, instead of giving presents to her, should contribute a sum of money to be given to the Listening Library.

She received many cards, telegrams and flowers, including one vase containing one hundred different flowers collected and arranged by a great friend.

All the great-grand-children, of whom there were eleven, were thrilled by the event and each sent their congratulations in their own way. Perhaps the best tribute to Alice Pollock is this verse written by a ten-year-old great-grandson:

"Now to-day you are a hundred
Never in your life have you ever blundered
Now you are a century old to-day
We wish you blessings along your way."

Marjorie Farrer.

PART ONE

The Days of Queen Victoria

CHAPTER ONE

MY FAMILY

I AM now over 102 years old and during this span of one life-time things have changed so rapidly that it is almost impossible to comprehend. Has it ever occurred before, I wonder, that in such a comparatively short period of time, one world—the world of my parents, could disappear and be almost forgotten and another world so different in every way take its place?

My father was the third son of Mr. Charles and Lady Jemima Wykeham-Martin of Leeds Castle, Kent. As a small boy he went to school by coach to a place near Swindon, then a swamp, where afterwards the Great Western had their workshop. In 1846, at the age of twelve, he fulfilled the necessary qualifications to serve as a Naval Cadet. These were that he "must be in good health and fit for service, that is, free from impediment of speech, defect of vision, rupture, or other physical inefficiency. He must be able to write English from dictation, and must be acquainted with the rules of Common Arithmetic, including the Rule of Three." He joined H.M.S. *Eurydice* for three years, in which he served first as a Naval Cadet, and then as a Midshipman. *Eurydice* was at that time commanded by Captain (later Admiral) Talavera Vernon Anson, a member of the same family as the famous eighteenth-century Admiral Lord Anson. During the Crimean War he saw service in different ships in the Baltic and a letter survives which he wrote to an aunt from H.M.S. *Neptune* on 7th September 1854: "As for myself and the Baltic Fleet," he wrote, "I quite blush whenever I think of it. If I had my way both Helsingfors and Cronstadt would have fallen long ago. As it is, we have only taken Alund in which we lost 2 men and 1 officer and 1 marine. One of the officers, a friend of mine, intercepted the mail and discovered that it was about to be relieved by some thousand troops, upon which information we attacked it immediately. There is one consolation; although we have not attacked any of the largest ports, we know that not a single Russian dares to show his nose outside to come and molest any of our dearest friends, and it is not unwillingness on the part of the young officers and sailors that prevents us burning St. Petersburg. I am quite sure if we were to go into Helsingfors tomorrow we should destroy the forts and burn the fleet and the same thing would happen if we attacked Cronstadt. I wish they would let us try. We would show them a *move*, I know. The cholera is raging very much among the French troops. They are losing 60 a day and have already lost 300 men. I think we have a good deal to fight against, since we have been up here; Russians, small-pox and cholera, a little dysentery and rheumatism. . . . I have just heard that we sail on the 15th of this month for England. I should think it is likely as the weather is getting worse every day and to say the truth I shall not be sorry for it, for lying here doing nothing in the fighting line is very monotonous work, to say the least of it."

From the Baltic he was sent to Panama in the Steam Sloop *Alert*, and this drastic change of climate affected his health so that he was invalided home in December 1859. He arrived at Leeds Castle, unannounced, and without his luggage. To his dismay he found a large house party staying at the Castle. In those days it would have been unthinkable to dine with guests without evening dress, and so he did not meet the guests until the next day, Thursday. Amongst them was Ann Katherine, the daughter of John Rolls. Apparently it was love at first sight, for on the following day, Friday, Father persuaded her to go on the moat with him where they spent the afternoon. By

Mother, 1861

Alice Wykeham-Martin, 4 years old

Sunday Father had made up his mind, and arranged with his cousin, Tom Flinn, to be ready to open the park gate leading to the church so that Father need not stay to do it. He then and there proposed and was accepted.

He now faced a dilemma; he was due to return to Panama, but, as everyone knows, it was one of the most unhealthy places in which to be stationed at that time, and he obtained a certificate from his doctor to say he was quite unfit to go there again. A correspondence ensued with the Admiralty, who unfortunately refused to accede to Father's request to send him elsewhere.

My Grandfather Rolls then refused to allow the marriage unless Father sent in his resignation. This was, I think, a most unfortunate decision, as my father was only twenty-eight. He would have liked to make the Navy his life career, and was described as a very promising officer. He retired with the Honorary rank of Captain in October 1860.

The marriage took place in January 1861, and the guests at the wedding prophesied Ann would be a widow within the year. How wrong they were! Father's health improved and he lived to the age of sixty-eight.

Father and Mother made their first home in the Isle of Wight. Father bought a small property situated on a hill above Newport. It consisted of a fair-sized house called "Staplers" in which they lived, with a very nice garden, a smaller house and two cottages. The smaller house was let, but in later years was lent to an old aunt of Father's, the last of her generation and rather eccentric. She kept every scrap of paper she had ever received, also all the papers of her three sisters. She was always afraid that *les domestiques* stole. She therefore deposited her jewellery and many £5 notes among her papers, where she thought they would be safe.

The place was packed with papers and after her death, Mother had to sort them with great care. I found Mother on one occasion in floods of tears, having read some of the old letters which had very disparaging remarks about herself from various relations.

Mother's family were wealthy, and she must have had a difficult time adjusting to a very different way of life from that to which she had been accustomed. She was a clever and ambitious woman, and would have liked Father to go into politics, but this he refused to do. His father, Charles Wykeham-Martin, was Liberal member for Newport, Isle of Wight, and also at one time member for Maidstone. Philip, his eldest brother, was Liberal member for Rochester, and eventually died in the House of Commons. Father was the only Conservative in his family.

Mother also wished that her eldest son would enter the Army, and the younger the Navy, neither of which ambitions was realised. Charles, the elder, after several attempts at other careers, ended by being a land agent, and Robert, the younger, failed for the Navy and became an electrical engineer.

Mother was very good-looking and must have been lovely when a girl. She had beautiful brown eyes and a good complexion, jet black hair with hardly a grey hair when she died at the age of seventy-four. She was known as "The Gazelle" among her friends. She was only 5 ft. 3 in. tall, but had a beautiful figure. In old age, when she became stout, she had great dignity. She was somewhat severe in manner and, although at heart very kind, she inspired considerable awe, and some people were rather frightened of her. She had generally little sense of humour, although the following story will show that it was not always absent.

A distant relation had come recently to the neighbourhood, and had come over to see Mother and to ask her about the neighbours. They had been talking for some time, and Mother, when she was bored, was apt to take little notice of what was said to her. Mrs. Mitchell asked her if a certain lady in our village had a husband. Mother's reply was, "No, we share one between us and we find it answers admirably." Mrs. Mitchell, quite horrified, drew her chair up to my mother and said, "Mrs. Wykeham-Martin, do you know what I asked you?"

Mother promptly answered, "Yes, you asked me if Mrs. Maskelyne has a library subscription." She was then told what the question had been, and was convulsed with laughter for a long time. She told her family and was often chaffed about it.

Rather a curious thing happened during the time my parents were living in the Isle of Wight. Mother was out walking with my brother Charlie in his perambulator, when she suddenly felt she must hurry home. The feeling was so strong that she immediately turned back. When she arrived at the house, a telegram awaited saying Uncle Fiennes (Father's brother) was dangerously ill, and asking my father to come at once. It was difficult to get to the mainland. There were few trains on the island and few boats to meet them. Father was out, but Mother sent someone to recall him, and in the meantime packed a suitcase and ordered a cab. When Father arrived he just had time to catch a train and boat. He arrived at his brother's house to find his brother so seriously ill that he was not expected to live through the night. He saw the doctor and asked him if he might spend the night alone with Fiennes, and also asked if it would be permissible to give him champagne. The doctor said that certainly he could do what he liked, as he thought the case quite hopeless, and that the patient would not live through the night.

Father took charge and sat by his brother, giving him sips of champagne occasionally, and most of the time praying earnestly that Fiennes' life might be spared for the period of six months. During the night a change took place, and he was so much better in the morning that the doctor was greatly surprised and thought that he might pull through. He did, and lived exactly six months. Father told me this story himself. He said he had a particular reason for wishing his brother to live another six months, but he did not tell me the reason.

On another occasion, when Mother was staying in London, she suddenly felt that she must go and see her father at once. This feeling was so intense that she went straight to Paddington, where she realised she had hardly any money with her. However, she and her family were well known on the line and she asked the station-master to lend her the money for her fare.

She did not tell me what reception she got, or what her family thought of her sudden and unexpected arrival. She merely told me that she found her father quite well and very pleased to see her. She stayed for a few days and then returned home, quite unable to account for her sudden impulsive action.

Three days afterwards, a loud scream was heard to come from the library, where my grandfather always rested after luncheon, and when people rushed to see what was the matter, they found him dead.

My parents continued to live at "Staplers" for four or five years. There was much social life, and they had many friends, but they found it very inconvenient living on the Island on account of fogs which often made it difficult to get to the mainland and delayed the arrival of letters and papers. Also I think Mother was anxious that Father should have some occupation. She wanted him to go into Parliament, but this he steadfastly refused to do. When they left the Island Father bought a house at Esher and he went into some business—I believe it was a plate glass company.

Two children were born at Esher, Eleanor and Theodora. My parents did not like Esher and my Father did not like business life.

CHAPTER TWO

COUNTRY LIFE

FATHER bought a house called "The Hill" at Purton, in Wiltshire, and lived there for thirty-six years until his death in 1903, and Mother stayed on until her death in 1912, after which the house was sold.

I was the first child to be born at Purton, on 2nd July 1868, followed by Annie, Katty, Robert and Sybil, at intervals of about two years.

Father settled down to country life, became a magistrate, a church warden, inspector of the Workhouse, and had a great deal to do with the Diocesan Society. He was elected a member of the first County Council of Wiltshire, when County Councils first came into existence in 1889. He attended all the political meetings and did a great deal in helping with the care of the poor. I think he had a useful and happy life.

He was a good sportsman and a very good shot, and was often asked to shoot with neighbours and relations. He filled his own cartridges, and one of our great delights was to be asked into the study to help him. We never ventured into the study except by special invitation, and we were always very excited on these occasions. There were two little measures, one for gunpowder and one for shot. A wad was added, then with a special tool the edges were turned down, and all was complete. We had to be most accurate in measuring quantities, and were not trusted with the final stage.

Father had the most extraordinary horror of snakes, and

on one occasion, when at a shooting party with Lord Bolingbroke at Lydiard Tregoze, one of the gamekeepers showed him an adder which had just been killed. This made Father so ill that he had to return home immediately.

The house in which we lived had been a boys' school. It certainly was not beautiful, but roomy and cheerful, facing the road. There was a good garden with a tennis lawn and a lower lawn with flower beds. These flower beds were always filled with geraniums, calceolarias and lobelia. Mother took all the geranium cuttings. On the upper lawn there was a fir tree in which at one time, much to my delight, a golden-crested wren built its nest and reared its family. There was a beautiful pink maytree with a seat under it, a very large kitchen garden and a greenhouse. There were poultry houses and a poultry yard, an orchard, pig styes, cow houses, a pond and four or five fields.

The ground floor of the house consisted of a drawing-room, dining-room, study, boudoir and a small business room, a pantry, a large kitchen, scullery and larder. Down below were the cellars, a big wine cellar and another big cellar where, until a new dairy was built, the milk and cream were kept. On one occasion of a dinner-party, there was a violent thunderstorm, and one of the ladies of the party insisted on going down to the cellar, where she remained until the storm was over. Whenever thunderstorms began, the servants covered looking-glasses all over the house and put away any knives that might be lying about. They were supposed to "draw the lightning".

On the first floor were my parents' bedroom and dressing-room, four other bedrooms (two double, two single). At the other end of the house was a large room, obviously the classroom of the school. It had large windows on both sides, with big window sills you could sit or lie on. Two of these windows looked into the stable yard, and these were divided off, making a passage and a small room and a lavatory. The remainder was divided into two rooms, used as a night nursery and a day nursery, each of which had a large window which overlooked the garden and a glorious view of the Cotswolds.

On the second floor was a large landing. There was a small room occupied later by the governess. A few steps on one side of the landing led to a large attic in which Theodora, Annie and I slept, and another room for two servants. A few steps from the other side of the landing led to two small rooms, one occupied by Eleanor and the other by the cook.

The domestic staff consisted of cook, kitchenmaid, parlourmaid, housemaid, nurse, nurserymaid, gardener and boy to help him, and a groom-coachman. I wonder how much an establishment of this sort would cost nowadays! I do not think Father's income was ever over £2,000.

One particular parlourmaid, whom both my parents thought the world of, had been with them for seventeen years, when one eventful day Father happened to want some of his old port. He had a small quantity in the inner cellar which he prized very much and only used on special occasions. A special occasion arose, and he went down into the cellar to get one of his precious bottles of port. On taking it up, he found that it had been disturbed and the cork was loose. He found that every bottle had been drained to the dregs. The only person with a key to the inner cellar, besides himself, was Netta the parlourmaid. It was then discovered that she quite frequently gave wine to her friends who came to the back door.

She wore Mother's silk stockings to shreds, and I believe she occasionally wore her dresses. She was, of course, dismissed, but it was a severe blow to my parents. We children disliked her intensely. She was always telling tales of us to our Mother and getting us into trouble, and we were very glad when she went. We could have told many tales about her!

Father was an extraordinarily kind man and most considerate of anyone he employed. There was a conservatory running along the side of the house which ended just by the pantry window. Father brought in a lot of mud on to the mat and, to save the maid, shook it outside. Being in the pantry at this time, I heard Netta, who was looking out of the window, remark, "Look at the old yawnups doing my work."

We had a wonderful old gardener, Golding by name. He looked after three or four cows, the pigs, poultry and ducks. He had the princely wage of 18/– a week. He brought eggs in as required every morning, and on several occasions there had been bad ones among them. His remark when rebuked for this was, "I can't see what they wants to make such a fuss about, I likes 'em a bit tasty meself." The progeny of the cows were taken into market once a year at Cricklade, when Golding regularly got drunk for the only time during the year. This was expected and condoned.

There was a cat on the premises that Golding was very fond of, and every morning the cat went to the gate to receive him when he arrived. As for us children, I am afraid we tormented our old gardener, playing all sorts of tricks on him in the cowshed and potting sheds.

Golding had a sad life as his wife was mentally afflicted, but he was absolutely devoted to her and tended her to the end. He had an only son who was a policeman in London, who often came down to see him and did a good deal for him. He lived to be a hundred, which was unusual in those days. Once he had a near escape, however. When driving the cows in to be milked, he had to pass a very large elm in the middle of a field. He and the cows had barely passed it one day, when it fell with a crash to the ground.

We had a favourite coachman, named William, who encouraged us in some of our mischievous games. There was great excitement when his uniform buttons, which were silver, were changed to gold. From that time on we always called him *le bouton d'or*. He married one of our kitchen-maids, and left our service and went into a factory in Swindon. When I was married, we had a special carriage from Purton to Swindon, and were shunted outside the station to await the express train from London to which we were to be attached and go on to Bath. While we were waiting William appeared and, climbing up into the carriage, talked to us until the train came in. His conversation was not very well suited to the occasion, as he told us, with tears in his eyes, of the death of his first wife, the kitchen-maid, and his present distress at the death of his second wife.

William taught us to ride. We kept a horse for the wagonette or the brougham, and a cob for Father's dog-cart. Father always had chestnut horses. We also had a pony called Bobby on which the children learned to ride.

We occasionally went riding with Father, who was a good horseman but very impatient. One day when I was riding with him, he hit Bobby with his whip, causing him to rear. I did not fall off, but I was thrown up into the air and landed on the pommel of the saddle. This was agonisingly painful, though I dare not complain. I had always hated riding and this incident completely spoilt my nerve. I was thankful when, soon afterwards, I was allowed to give up riding—not because I was afraid of it, but because Father thought I rode so badly that it was not worth teaching me.

None of the family cared about riding except Charlie, who later in life hunted fairly regularly, and Eleanor who rode a good deal with Father but gave it up when she married.

I well remember the little riding habit which we all wore in turn. It was a long grey skirt, which came down over our feet, and a loose grey jacket. Under this we wore a white bodice. Eleanor had a smart riding outfit, and she also had a beautiful little whip with a gold handle, given to her by Uncle Philip Wykeham-Martin.

Mother, when visiting amongst the poor people of the parish, took them nourishing food and sometimes "Tarragona", a very light port, which she took in medicine bottles to various old people, by whom it was very much appreciated. She also kept an eye on the foster-children boarded out from the Workhouse. These children were supplied with a good outfit of clothing, a great deal of which was made by us children. They were also given a Bible and Prayer Book.

Mother was particularly fond of a nice woman, a Mrs. Bunce, who was very poor, with many children, and very glad of the extra money allowed her for the foster-child. Mother noticed when she was visiting that the little girl in question was dressed in rather tattered clothes and not too clean. She asked Mrs. Bunce why she had on such ragged clothes and asked to see her wardrobe. Mrs. Bunce had to confess that she had pawned or sold all the good clothes, and felt the child would be happier dressed just like the other children, their wardrobe having been stretched to accommodate her. The child was devoted to Mrs. Bunce and very happy, and somehow it was arranged that, despite her failings, she should keep the child.

As time went on Mother found herself unable to get to the outlying parts of the parish where the poorer people lived, and a bright idea occurred to my Father that shafts should be attached to a bathchair which we had, to which Bobby could be harnessed and then Mother could go her rounds without undue fatigue.

On one occasion, when she had gone to Pedenhill, about four miles from our home, she went into a cottage where she was only going to stay for a few minutes. She left Bobby at the side of the road without tying him up securely. Unfortunately, at this moment the hounds appeared in full cry across the field. This was too much for Bobby. He rushed up the bank and through the hedge, breaking the shafts and harness, hoping to join the chase. This he was unable to do, encumbered with the remains of shafts and harness, so he trotted off for home. There was great consternation in the village as he passed through, and, when he arrived home, terror as to what had happened to Mother. The brougham was immediately got ready and they went off to find her. Half-way to Pedenhill they met a boy who beckoned to them to stop. He was on his way to "The Hill" to say that Mother was in his mother's cottage and quite safe. Mother was none the worse and continued driving about the village in the pony carriage when it had been mended. When Mother gave up her visiting, Bobby had boots fitted and was used to draw the lawn mower.

Mother had many bright ideas which never came to anything. Whenever she went away for a visit, she always came back with some wonderful new ideas. On one occasion she had heard that newspaper kept people warm, and she had newspapers put between the blankets on our beds. I hated it—they rustled every time one moved. They did not last long. After another visit, to friends in Lancashire, she brought home clogs for the whole family. They were most uncomfortable, but we had to wear them.

At one time she thought she was going to make a lot of money rearing chicks by using incubators. The day-old chicks were put in an incubator, which in those days was heated by an oil lamp. It was important the temperature be kept even, which meant constant attention to the heater. This I think was neglected, so the whole project proved a failure.

There were some poor people in Purton, which was a large parish, but I think there was no real destitution or want. Edith Veysey, one of the vicar's daughters, a year older than me and a great friend of mine, spent her whole time going round and making friends with everyone. I think she knew every cottage and the name of every occupant. There was no "keeping up with the Jones's" in those days, and when any trouble occurred the neighbours all rallied round, giving of their precious time and often, I think, giving a great deal more than they could afford to give, willingly and without grudging it.

The one terror the old people had was of being taken to "The House" (Workhouse). They did everything they could to remain in their own homes, or in relations' houses, until want of attention and time to give it made it inevitable that they should go to "The House". One did not hear loneliness talked about in those days as it is now. I think the lonely time came in "The House" where in gloomy surroundings they could only look forward to dreary and monotonous days away from their kith and kin and all the gossip of the village, relieved only on visiting days, which occurred once a week.

Mother ran the nurses for North Wiltshire, organised Mothers' meetings and also young men's Bible classes. She built a Cottage Hospital with a legacy she had left her by an old aunt. The hospital was built in one of our fields. It was kept going by voluntary subscriptions for a good many years. It did good work until a larger hospital was built at Swindon and our hospital was then turned into a Home for convalescent, crippled children from London. As we grew up, Father found the expense too great and it was given up as a Home, and let as a private house.

There was a celebrated shop, Harford's, in Purton. It was large, with an enormous glass window frontage, and must have been capable of holding a vast quantity of merchandise. They issued their own tokens. There was a house attached to the shop, in which lived Miss Harford, the owner, and a Miss Knight. All the work was done by Miss Knight, as Miss Harford was too grand to appear in the shop. At Christmas time, it was the custom for the trades people to give presents to their customers. The wine merchant always sent us a box of wonderful biscuits, and a box of prunes.

On Boxing Day the grocer, butcher and several farmers had clubbed together to have a small shoot. The grocer supplied a large luncheon and, I believe, champagne. I think the shoot consisted chiefly of rabbits and an occasional hare, and I doubt very much whether they would have been capable of shooting birds. However, the shoot took place and they came home in a good-humoured state, having shot the grocer—fortunately at some distance. However, he had many pellets in his face and neck, and was on view for days in the shop, quite delighted to show himself off. I well remember going to see him.

There were few means of getting about when I was a girl. There were a few trains from Purton Station, otherwise the carrier's cart went into Swindon once a week. The Old Town was the shopping centre, and there were some quite good shops. It adjoined the New Town, which was almost entirely workmen's houses.

A great many people in our village were employed at the Swindon Railway works and the men used to walk to work the shortest way, about five miles, along the canal towpath. Father eventually persuaded the railway authorities to run a special train from Purton Station to the works at six o'clock in the morning and back at six o'clock in the evening.

The Great Western Railway was built in 1835 by Isambard Kingdom Brunel, the engineer and bridge builder, with a broad gauge of 7 ft., but other railways used the narrow gauge. Owing to the difficulties of changing coaches on to the lines of the other railways, the Great Western finally abandoned the broad gauge in 1892 and adopted the narrower one. The Swindon Railway workshops made and repaired the magnificent steam locomotives and the rails.

For many years the Swindon people had an agreement for all trains from Paddington to stop at Swindon which, in consequence, was quite an important place. The station was large, and there was a big assembly room there. Mother took us for a treat to see over the Swindon Railway workshops. We found it intensely interesting and I have always loved the magnificent steam engines. The broad-gauge engines of the Great Western were a beautiful sight.

The really thrilling moment arrived when we were shown the Nasmyth hammer. It was large and could come down with tremendous force, but for our edification Father's watch was borrowed and put down on the ground. To our horror, the hammer then slowly descended. We felt quite certain that Father's watch would be smashed to pieces. However, this enormous hammer was brought down so gently that, after just touching the watch, it stopped—much to our intense relief—and Father reclaimed his watch.

Mother was as much impressed as we children were. When she had read his Autobiography, she wrote to Nasmyth, and received the following very charming letter in return:

> Hammerfield,
> Penshurst,
> Kent.
> April 14, 1883.

Dear Madam,

I am most gratified by your very kind and valued approval of my attempt at an autobiography of my busy and much enjoyed life. Altho' I naturally feel the accelerating oncome of old age I still endeavour to continue those pleasant pursuits which have so long afforded me enjoyment and kept up the lively interest I take in the study of Nature and art.

Again thanking you most sincerely for your kind and valued letter,

> Believe me I am
> Yours very respectfully,
> JAMES NASMYTH

Mrs. A. K. Wykeham-Martin.

Travelling in the eighteen-eighties on the railway was certainly not comfortable. The carriages were divided into compartments complete in themselves, with no access to any other part of the train. The trains were bitterly cold and the windows covered with frost which made it impossible to see outside. The only means of warming the carriages was to obtain from the porter a metal foot-warmer, filled with hot water. These were soon cooled by the draught under the door, but when you stopped at any big station there were truck-loads brought down the platform, and the porter took away your cold one and gave you a fresh hot one for which you paid sixpence The railways had three classes of carriages—first, second and third. Valets and ladies' maids travelled second. When we went to stay at large country houses we were met at the station by a smart footman. Father could not afford first-class tickets for us girls, so our one aim was to get out of the train with our belongings before the footman saw that we had been travelling second calss.

There were no corridors on trains until they were first introduced by the Great Western in 1890. A few compartments had lavatories attached. These carriages were much sought after and it was often difficult to find an empty place in one. This was sometimes inconvenient on long distance trains. On one occasion, when we were going to London, one of my aunts, Georgie Chester-Master, was travelling by the same train, though in a different carriage. The train was a non-stop to London, but to everyone's surprise it slowed down as we approached Reading, finally drawing up by the platform. Everyone rushed to the windows to see what was going on.

There was quite a commotion on the platform, among the station-master and various officials and porters. They ran down the train to find the compartment where the communication cord had been pulled, probably expecting serious illness or even death. But after a short interval my aunt emerged from the carriage, quite calm and dignified. She was escorted by the station-master to the ladies' waiting-room. After a short pause she returned, again escorted by the station-master, to her carriage, quite undisturbed by the commotion she had caused and the amused faces of the other passengers. As far as I know it led to no unpleasantness for her and was, I suppose, considered as an "emergency".

Another instance! A very large "do" was being held at Blenheim—I think a wedding to which all Society was going. A train full of guests stopped on the way at a station for a few minutes and a well-known lady got out and went to the ladies' waiting-room. Hearing the whistle she hurried out, but unfortunately for her the door swung to and caught her dress firmly in it. Another penny was required to release her and, though she searched frantically in her bag, none was forthcoming. She called for help without avail, and the train sped on. Her friends were concerned as to what had happened to her, and at the party there were many enquiries and rumours. Eventually the story got about, much to the amusement of Society but *not* to the lady in question.

When I was about seventeen I went to stay with a friend to whom I had been bridesmaid. At the end of the visit they saw me off from Peterborough by an express train which did not stop till it arrived in London. They took care to see me into a carriage where I should come to no harm, second-class and empty except for a middle-aged couple, obviously man and wife, seated at the other end. Goodbyes were said and the train started. It was a hot day and the carriage was insufferably stuffy, both windows being shut. At that time it was customary for the person occupying the corner seat facing the engine to have command of the window, though naturally with polite reference to their neighbours and opposite number. I had no one sitting opposite me, and I let the window down and settled down to read a book.

Almost immediately the man came across the carriage and pulled my window up with a bang, with no reference whatever to me. I was furious and as he went back to his seat let the window down again. This proceeding was repeated several times. Then I got tired of it and placed my arm over the edge of the window. The man, undeterred, came back, but I was ready for him. I looked him straight in the face and said, "If you dare touch me I will give you in charge for assault when we reach London." This apparently settled him, for he returned to his wife and for the rest of the journey they put up their umbrella and sat behind it all the way. When we arrived in London and their friends came to greet them, I heard them denouncing the horrible modern girl they had travelled with, and they could not imagine what the world was coming to. So I became a modern girl of that generation!

On arrival at a London station there would be plenty of four-wheelers awaiting hire. Most of these cabs were shabby, badly-sprung and often dirty vehicles, their floor covered with straw. The horses were in poor condition, and did not go at any pace. There were a few cabs which were smart, with good upholstery and quite good horses. Outside the station there were always a lot of loafers, one of whom attached himself to one's cab and ran the whole way to the destination with the intention of getting a tip for unloading the luggage, which he would start doing almost before the cab had stopped. I always tried to prevent their going into the house, as they were often dirty and probably not too honest. If they were unable to accomplish their aim they became terribly abusive and were very hard to get rid of. When travelling with children or several people with too much luggage for a four-wheeler, one hired a small 'bus to meet one at the station.

CHAPTER THREE

THE SCHOOLROOM

As time went on and the family increased, it became necessary for the older children to have a governess. The day nursery was turned into a schoolroom and a boudoir on the ground floor was then used as a day nursery. This room joined and opened into the drawing-room. The door in the drawing-room was closed and a large cupboard made in the recess.

Among my earliest memories is that of having my photograph taken when I was four years old. It was taken on the lawn. Charlie was resplendent in brand-new clothes which I think must have been his first knickerbocker suit. Theodora and I wore white piqué frocks. We were shy and, certainly as far as I was concerned, felt rather frightened. I was frightened both of the photographer and of the camera.

I also remember, when I was within a month of my fifth birthday, the birth of my younger brother. We realised there was a good deal of excitement going on in the house and they said Mrs. Freeman had arrived. To our surprise, Mrs. Freeman was installed in Father's dressing-room which led into Mother's bedroom and Father moved into the spare room across the passage. We thought it odd but did not bother any more about it. Next morning we were told that Mrs. Freeman had brought a new baby—a boy—and we were all taken to Mother's room to see it. There was a lot of talk as to what the name of the boy was to be. Finally, Robert Fiennes was decided upon. I thought the baby ugly and I was very bored. Three years later, when I was eight, Mrs. Freeman came again and this time brought a little girl, Sybil Elizabeth. The nurse, whose idol was Robert, was seen to kick the basinette from one end of the nursery to the other, exclaiming: "It's an ugly red-headed little devil!"

It is interesting to note the difference in the present day, when a child of four would be fully cognisant of all matters concerning the birth of another member of the family. At eight years old I happily received the news, still with a firm belief in Mrs. Freeman.

Mother had the village doctor for the births of her children, and his fee was £5.

Our old Nurse Howes was a Norfolk woman. She was full of superstitions which we learnt from her. If on your daily walk a flock of sheep came in sight and they were going away from you, all was well, but if you should meet a flock of sheep coming towards you, you had better turn home at once or it would be very unlucky.

Two spoons occurring accidentally when laying the table or on a saucer indicated an engagement of marriage. Two knives crossed on a table were a certain sign of a quarrel unless you immediately removed the top one, when you might avert a disaster. If you curtsied eight times to the moon, wishing at the same time, you were certain to get your wish. To find out the initial of the man you were to marry, you must peel an apple without breaking it. It must be the whole apple. You then, carefully, lifted the peel, put it three times round your head and threw it on the floor. The initial would then appear.

She often threatened us with the Devil and I felt I would like to see him. She said that if you went, when dusk had fallen, into a room by yourself and looked into a looking-glass, you would see him looking over your shoulder. This I was determined to do and one evening, just as a lamp had been brought into the schoolroom, I crept out and, shaking with fear, went down the long passage to our bedroom. I opened the door and went in. I got half-way across the room when I was overcome with terror and rushed back to the warmth and light of the schoolroom. I did not tell anyone of my adventure and I have never tried to see the Devil since.

To dream of one's young man could be induced in the following manner. As you were getting into bed, using your dressing slippers for the purpose, you would say "Placing these shoes in the form of a T, hoping this night my true love to see."

Breaking a looking-glass was supposed to be frightfully unlucky. I broke one very soon after my engagement to be married and I do not think anyone could ever have been more happily married. If you see a piebald horse and can refrain from thinking of his tail you will get your wish.

Nurse Howes was a great character and a good nurse, but she did not have an easy time for we were naughty children and she did not realise that we were able to elude her (when she would otherwise have found us out) by a habit she had of sniffing loudly. At the first sound of a sniff we always disappeared. She had a young man—or perhaps I should say an old man! He was a tall, thin, cadaverous person, always dressed in black and always wore a rather dilapidated tall hat. I think he was something to do with the undertaker. We never knew his real name, but we nicknamed him "Hud-me-Dud". Through a hole in the blind at the bedroom window, we used to watch Howes and her fiancé at the front gate and we would all get safely back to bed before she came in. She did not marry until she was fairly old. She was married from our house and when the governess went up to talk to her the night before the wedding, Howes, who appeared in anything but good spirits, remarked: "There is no fool like an old fool."

She had quite a nice house in the village and I went to tea with her several times. But soon after her marriage she became very ill and died.

The governess Mother engaged was called Miss Taylor.

She and her brother and sister lost their father at an early age and their mother died soon after. They were brought up in a home for the children of officers killed on active service, where they remained until ready to earn their own living. Our Miss Taylor was, I think, about nineteen or twenty. We were very fond of her. She was a strict disciplinarian, and what she knew I think she taught well, but her teaching had to include every subject. The three eldest children, Charlie, Eleanor and Theodora, went into the schoolroom. I was very eager to get in there too, and I was afterwards told that I used to sit on the mat outside the schoolroom door for long periods of time, hoping that I would be able to get in. I was about four years old when Miss Taylor took pity on me and allowed me to go in and have lessons with the others.

I remember my first lessons quite well. I can see the copy books with the lines beginning with strokes and then letters faintly printed, which we had to copy over. The next process was a line of letters with blank spaces beneath in which we had to copy the letters, and so on to words and sentences. I think this produced good writing, as seen in some old letters which Mother kept. Great importance was attached to the way one held one's pen, and many a smack I received for not holding it properly.

Miss Taylor punished rather severely. She kept a long brown wooden ruler (I can see it now) by the side of her on the table at meal times. Should any child rest her hand or hands on the table, a sharp rap on the knuckles soon made them disappear; and even now, if I find my hands on the table, I instantly withdraw them. We also had what we called Thimble Pie. The governess had a thimble on one finger and used to rap us on the head with it if we were not sitting up straight enough!

We were often whipped, but I do not think we ever resented being punished, as long as we considered it just. On one occasion when out walking, I was looking for snail shells and got behind the rest of the party. They hid from

me and went back home by a different way. I was frightened
and hurried home, going directly up to the governess's
room where I apologised most humbly. She accepted my
apology and I thought all was well, but she put down her
book and said: "This will not let you off your punishment,"
and gave me a good whipping. I was furious about this for
a long time as I considered it very unjust.

On another occasion I spotted a wren's nest above the
swill-tub in one of the sheds. I proceeded to climb up the
side to reach the nest, and fell in. My condition was
indescribable, and it was quite impossible to conceal what
had happened, so I had to confess before I could get a
change of garments and I was severely reprimanded. My
brothers and sisters teased me for a long time about it, as
they declared I had been trying to find something to eat
and in that way had fallen in.

We were taught all sorts of needlework: sewing, hem-
ming, running, backstitch, herring boning, cross-stitch;
how to put in a gusset, to mitre a corner, to do blanket-
stitch, button-holes, crewel work, French knots, darning,
fine tucks and gathering, as well as knitting and crochet.

There was a way of making scarves with a "Peggy",
which was a thick piece of wood with a hole in the middle
and little pegs all round the edges. You wound the wool
round, looped it over, threaded the wool again and so on,
until you made a long scarf.

We had to darn our stockings and mend our clothes. We
made handkerchief-sachets, nightdress cases, and embroidered tray cloths as presents. I always enjoyed doing these
very much. At an early age we learned to work on canvas
and made kettle-holders. When darning, we used a wooden
egg or mushroom to hold the work, and had to make a
pattern over the hole with threads of wool in and out
alternately, making a neat repair.

All our sheets were made at home, and we spent long
afternoons of hand-sewing the hems and sometimes, with
old sheets, joining sides to middles. Mother did a great deal

of crewel work, and made some rather beautiful panels of Tudor patterns for the doors between the dining-room and drawing-room.

In the winter we attended dancing classes which were held in the Assembly Room at Swindon. To us it was always a terrifying event. The dancing-master was the old-fashioned type with long hair, and he wore knee breeches and tail coat. He had a beautiful lady to help him. He played a fiddle and she played the piano. She was, I believe, considered not quite proper! The room had chairs all round the walls, and on these the respective mothers and nannies sat. The children were let into the room one by one, and each child had to walk the length of the room and curtsey to the dancing-master. We were severely criticised by him for our deportment and carriage, and occasionally sent back to do it all over again—a nerve-racking experience.

When Annie and Katty came into the schoolroom it became necessary to have a second governess to teach the younger ones. This governess was named Miss Mew; most appropriately, she later married a Mr. Catt!

About this time, Father decided to build on to the schoolroom end of the house. Below the schoolroom was the kitchen and leading from that a larder and an enormous scullery, which had an old-fashioned pump at one end, and hot and cold water laid on to a sink at the other. I cannot remember the floor above the scullery, but I think it was rather ramshackle. In any case, it was pulled down, and on the ground floor Father made a nice larder and dairy, leaving the rest of the scullery empty. He put a top floor with four bedrooms (two double and two single), hot and cold water taps in the passage and a lavatory. A cold water and a hot water tank were installed in the roof. Before this the hot water tank was over the scullery sink and that was connected with the pantry, the only places where you could obtain hot water. The tanks in the new building provided cold and hot water upstairs for the first time. Before that everything had been fetched from the scullery. All the water in the tanks was pumped up from the well which was situated in the scullery. The pumping up took place every morning and evening.

We were fond of messing about in the building when the men had gone to their dinner, their dinner hour coinciding with a break in our lessons. We messed about, taking putty and playing with their tools and they complained. We were, in consequence, forbidden to go near the building at any time. This, however, did not deter us and one morning we went round to see how things were getting on. The roof was on and we could see that one of the floors was beginning to be laid. Eleanor announced her intention of going up to inspect. We stood watching her while she made a rather perilous ascent up a shaky ladder and over several obstacles. However, at last she got into the room and proceeded to walk along the rafters when, to our horror, she slipped and fell through the rafters, being caught by her clothes and her arms were quite free. The lower part of her body and legs looked funny to us, especially as she began kicking furiously imploring us to help her. This we could not possibly do. If we had got up the same way she did we should probably have met the same fate. She could not heave herself up and implored us to get something below that we could stand on and possibly push her up. We were convulsed with laughter and she got more and more furious with us. However, time was getting on, the workmen would soon be back and we were due in the schoolroom. We did not want to be caught and Eleanor did not want to be discovered in that position by the workmen. With one supreme effort she heaved herself up and managed to scramble down just as they were arriving and we all skedaddled off to the schoolroom. We were not found out on that occasion. I also remember Annie being caught by her skirt in much the same way on a tree. In that case it was possible to help her and she was got down without accident.

When I was about eleven Miss Taylor became very ill

and it was arranged that she should go to her brother
Oscar for a long rest, after which it was hoped that she
would be able to return. She became rapidly worse and
they diagnosed Bright's disease, with no hope of her
ultimate recovery. Oscar Taylor was moving house and
Father and Mother offered to have Miss Taylor back at
Purton while this was taking place. She was very ill and a
bedroom was prepared for her downstairs in the boudoir.
She was soon unable to sit up except in bed. I was fond of her
and constantly went in to see her. In the evenings, when the
others went out to play, I went and sat with her, reading
her letters and listening to many confidences. She was, I
think, fond of me, and told me stories of her love affairs
and many other things. Then a sad thing happened. Owing
I now realise to her illness, she took a violent dislike to me
and abused me to every one. I was terribly upset by this.
She went back to her brother's house, where she died soon
afterwards.

After this Mother thought it a good idea for us to have
a foreign governess, and she got a Miss Hirsch, a French-
woman. She was only with us a short time and we disliked
her. She was dismissed suddenly, after news of her character
had been sent home by my brother Charlie, who was then
in France, and had met someone who knew her.

The new governess was to have one of the single rooms
and Eleanor the other. I had one of the double rooms with
Theodora; Annie and Katty slept in the other.

We then had a Miss de la Valette, a descendant of the
great de la Valette family. Some of the family had escaped
to Germany during the French Revolution, where they had
become naturalised, and Miss de la Valette was brought up
as a German. We loved her and she, I think, was very fond
of us, but unfortunately she had no control over us and we
led her a dreadful life. I think the climax was reached when
on one occasion she was away for the day, and we locked
Theodora in Miss de la Valette's bedroom with a sewing-
machine. She machined all the sheets together and her

nightdress—the hems, sleeves and neck. After this Miss de la Valette gave notice.

Mother said she would get a strict governess in future, and she engaged a Miss Iseke, a German. We detested her. Unfortunately, she attained a great deal of influence over our Mother, and made mischief between her and us. She was eventually established, when we had all left the school-room, as a companion to Mother, where she remained until Mother's death.

Miss Iseke punished a good deal, and Eleanor was subjected to much severer punishment than the rest of the family. I think Miss Iseke disliked her, and made mischief between her and Mother. On one occasion she persuaded her to have Eleanor locked in her room, which was an attic and cold. She was to be fed on bread and water for a week and to see no one. She became ill and the doctor had to be sent for. On enquiry as to what had happened, he was furious, ordering her to be put to bed and kept warm, and to be given good food. One lung was slightly touched.

A hundred lines in playtime after lessons was quite a common punishment, also being sent to bed after tea on lovely sunny days. I had a basket for holding string, to which I attached a long string and let it down from my bedroom window to Robert, who was then small. He filled it with delicious ripe gooseberries, which I hauled up and devoured with great satisfaction. It was not such fun in the winter, when we had no light.

As Miss Iseke's influence increased with Mother, we saw less of her. Miss Iseke was always trying to take the position of eldest daughter of the house. We always called Mother "Mum", and to our great rage Miss Iseke called her "Mumchen".

CHAPTER FOUR

RELIGION

FATHER and Mother were sincerely religious. They were great admirers of Mr. Wilkinson, a well-known rector at St. Peter's, Eaton Square, afterwards Bishop of Truro. They were what was called in those days Broad Church, as distinct from Low or High Church. We were taught to say our prayers and we were brought up on the books, *Line upon Line* and *Precept upon Precept*, of which we had a portion read to us every morning. We had to say our Catechism and learn a Collect to be said on Sunday morning before church, and sometimes a psalm as well. Grace was said before and after every meal.

We had prayers before breakfast at which we had hymns, accompanied by an harmonium. On one occasion when Theodora and I were left at home alone (this was when we were grown-up, seventeen or eighteen), we thought it right to have prayers as usual. Theodora read the prayers quite successfully and I played the hymns. Unfortunately, I did not see the repetition mark at the end of the first line of the first hymn. The hymn began, "Great God, what do I see and hear." What we heard was the maids singing at the top of their voices on the wrong line of music, and I was almost in tears, not understanding what had happened. I collapsed after the first verse, and that was the end.

We went regularly to church in the neighbouring village of Lydiard, the services in our own parish being at that time extreme Low Church. The parson preached in a black gown and the length of the sermon was usually an hour or more. We seldom attended the parish church, but on one occasion when we did, after nearly an hour's discourse, the parson said, "There is not time to follow the Israelites through their journey." "Thank the Lord," said absent-minded Major Prower in a loud voice, and jumped up. Realising what he had said, he sat down again hastily on his tall hat, which his son had slipped on to his seat. It made a loud report like a shot gun. Suppressed laughter all round, and we felt it made up for the long dreary sermon we had listened to. We walked over a mile to church, and in Lent went to services on Wednesdays and Fridays.

We always looked forward to meeting a number of young men who were being tutored by a Mr. MacKnight at Lydiard. Mr. MacKnight was very Low Church. Our governess was in love with the assistant tutor who lived in the lodge of Mr. MacKnight's house, and she used to go in there to breakfast on her way back from early service. I am afraid she was much in love with him, but he went abroad and she never saw him again.

Just at the end of Purton village was a pond and outside the church at Lydiard was another pond. There were two swans who spent their time partly on one pond, and partly on the other. When they were getting old they often walked quite a long way along the road between the ponds, and unfortunately one day a careless driver killed the pen. The cob was found standing by the side of her, apparently in great distress, and it was quite a long time before they were able to remove the dead body. The cob went into the reeds on the edge of the pond, where three days afterwards he was found dead: we said he died of a broken heart.

After the old Low Church parson died and the clergyman at the church which we attended left, we went to our parish church. Here a curious custom used to be kept up on Good Friday. Long ago money had been left to provide a loaf of bread and sixpence for each woman and a shilling for each man who came to church on Good Friday. The bread was stacked in the porch. From early morning the poorer people came in crowds. The church was crammed. Most of the congregation had not been to church during the year. The parson received £1 for preaching the sermon. He gave them their money's worth, seldom preaching for less than an hour. This Good Friday service, to which we had to go, was a real penance.

Theodora and I had a pleasant surprise after one of those services. We always went on Good Friday afternoon to the copse not far from the church to pick primroses for the Easter decorations. On this occasion we were asked by some rather eccentric people who lived at a big house close by the church if we would like to have luncheon with them, instead of going home and then coming all the way back to pick the flowers. We accepted, and imagine our surprise when, instead of the salt fish which we would have had at home, we were regaled with an excellent luncheon and champagne! We had never tasted champagne before—we were delighted.

We were taught to deny ourselves something during Lent. I always think this scheme which we carried out was the best one I know of. We had large tin biscuit boxes provided, and every morning we solemnly deposited the two lumps of sugar allowed for our bread and milk into the tin boxes. At the end of Lent it was weighed and Mother paid us for it. We sent the money to the Kilburn Orphanage.

We were not allowed to play games on Sunday. In the afternoons we girls, when old enough, went for a walk alone. All grown-up women went to their beds and to sleep. The men went for walks. In the evening we sang hymns, played by Mother on the harmonium. In later years Mother was not so strict, and my younger sisters as they grew up were allowed to play tennis and croquet on Sunday afternoon.

Mother's eldest sister, Mrs. Harcourt-Mitchell, a great churchwoman, was Eleanor's godmother and Eleanor was sent for to the drawing room to be lectured and prayed with. Our elders were great letter writers. They had a horrid habit of crossing and re-crossing their letters. True their writing was, in those days, more or less of an art, but the crossing made them very difficult to decipher. They wrote great details of their home life to their sisters, often with complaints of the behaviour of their children, upon which the aunts, who were often also Godmothers, would take up their pens and write the most severe lectures to their Godchildren. I objected very much to this sort of thing, and was very angry when I received a letter from Aunt Elizabeth reprimanding me very severely about some quarrel with Mother, who had apparently complained of me. I wrote back to my aunt, saying: "Dear Aunt Elizabeth. As you have only heard one side of the argument, I do not consider you are competent to judge it. Your affectionate niece, Alice." I believe this letter was sent round to all the aunts, but I never received another letter from Aunt Elizabeth.

I always look upon Father as one of the really good men that I have known. He was extraordinarily kind, full of fun, and had a knack of telling a good story better than anyone that I have ever met. It was said of him that he not only knew every man, woman and child in the village, but every cat and dog as well! I remember his saying to me once that one should always pass the time of day with everyone one met. He was speaking of the country, of course. He always used to say that a friendly greeting might help to cheer up someone who was feeling depressed. I took his advice, and have always talked to all and sundry. On one occasion I sat down on a seat in Kensington Gardens next to a rather dirty, miserable-looking old woman. I made a remark to her about the flowers and she looked at me in some surprise. I said something else to her and she soon began to talk, and eventually I heard the whole story of her life, which was a very sad one.

Father was a straight, upright, honest, English gentleman. He endeavoured to do his duty in the station of life into which God had called him. He took people at their face value and made the best of them. I am sure he never disliked anyone. He hated gossip and put a stop at once to any sign of it. He was a contented and, I think, a happy man. There were many rich relations in the family and he often said: "The rich relations have large incomes and small families. I have a small income and a large family, and am happier than any of them." He was devoted to Mother and very proud of his children.

I think I can explain Father's rule for his life in the following words which he often quoted; I do not know where they came from, but I believe from an old song:

> "Do yer duty,
> Love mercy,
> Be gentle and kind,
> Do yer duty."

It is not difficult to understand that Father, owing to his character, was easily taken in. I will give an instance or two of this happening.

One evening, on returning home on a wet dark night, he stumbled across a prostrate body. On examination it proved to be a man lying unconscious. He realised that the man was alive and quickly fetched help. They took him to the Cottage Hospital, where he was put to bed and given restoratives and soon regained consciousness. He was shabbily dressed, his clothes were almost threadbare, but he was scrupulously clean. He was also shaven. Father went up the next morning to find out about him. The doctor had been, and said he could find no organic disease. The man was in a poor and emaciated state, he only wanted good nourishment and rest to put him to rights.

It was soon realised that he was an educated man and an agreeable one. Matron took a great fancy to him, and Father brought him constantly down to the house for a chat and a glass of sherry, and found him quite interesting to talk to. The only information he gave about himself was that he had had misfortune after misfortune and had been reduced to his present condition with no means except tramping the roads. He said he was on his way to London, where he hoped to find friends and some relations and possibly get work. He remained for some time at the hospital, regaining his strength before being pronounced fit enough to be discharged. Everybody was sorry he was going and some of the villagers had been interested in the case. A small contribution had been got up, and Mother gave him some shirts of Father's and an overcoat. He was also provided with boots and some socks.

Several months afterwards Father received a visit from the village policeman. He said he had heard from the Reading police who were making enquiries about a man whom the police had found unconscious in the road and had taken to hospital. His shirts were marked with the name Cornwallis Wykeham-Martin, and an envelope addressed to the Matron of the Cottage Hospital, Purton, led to their enquiries. Did the police at Purton know anything of a Cornwallis Wykeham-Martin? The policeman at once came to Father to ask if it were a relation of his, and Father explained that the man was no relation, and that Mother had not cut the name-tapes from the shirts which she had given him. The police were able to find out a good deal about the man, and arrived at the conclusion that his degradation had been brought about through gambling. Father never heard any more about him, but he still remained trustful in spite of frequent disillusionment.

And now for a rather more disagreeable episode. Our vicar had been very ill and had to have a long convalescence. During this time a "guinea pig" was procured to come every Saturday to Monday and conduct the services. This was Dr. Clutterbuck, a member of a well-known family. He made great friends with Father, who had long conversations with him—very often about religious matters. He was a good preacher and Father liked his sermons so much that he got Dr. Clutterbuck to allow him to have them copied for him. I am not quite sure whether it was

during his ministrations at Purton or afterwards that
Dr. Clutterbuck was arrested when getting out of a train
with his mistress. He had on his visits at various vicarages
persuaded the vicars or their wives to let him invest or re-
invest their capital. He had been leading a double life,
keeping a mistress in one place and visiting his wife, who
lived at Bath and had several children and was entirely
unconscious of his practices. He was duly punished, I
think by a long term of imprisonment. Father was very
upset about the whole business, and Dr. Clutterbuck's
sermons met their end on a bonfire.

On another occasion Father was let down by an enter-
tainer. A man arrived in the village and came to see Father,
telling him he was giving an entertainment at the Institute
on Saturday and that he was a mesmerist and would
demonstrate his mesmeric powers with some of the village
lads. He said that, in going about the village, he had heard
of our Cottage Hospital and he proposed to give half the
proceeds of the entertainment to the hospital. Father was
delighted, had a long talk with him, gave him a whisky and
soda and promised that he and his family would attend in
full force. Father told everybody what a nice man this
mesmerist was and that he hoped that they would attend
the entertainment. In consequence the hall was crammed to
overflowing. I thought it a horrid performance. He mes-
merised some of the village lads and made them do all sorts
of extraordinary things. The next day being Sunday the
mesmerist came to church and sat just behind us. I was
afraid he might mesmerise us and was glad to get out of
church. On Monday morning Father waited in, expecting
the man to turn up with the donation for the hospital.
He waited until after 12 noon and then went out to enquire
as to his whereabouts. He had left early in the morning,
leaving no donation for the hospital and was never heard
of again.

In his capacity as a magistrate, Father had to pay visits
of inspection to the large Workhouse which was situated

in our village. He went there once a month and should, I think, have gone round on his own to receive any complaints from the inmates. However he was fond of the Workhouse-master, who apparently took a great interest in everyone in the "House" and always suggested going round with Father. This, of course, prevented any complaints being made. Somehow the facts about Mr. Jones, the Workhouse-master came to light. He lived quite a luxurious life, drank heavily, kept the unfortunate inmates without fires in very cold weather and gave them poor food. There were many other accusations about his cruelty. A great deal of the allowance he had for the necessities of the "House" went into his own pocket. Again Father had been too trusting. However none of these things stopped his trust in human nature and he remained the dear, simple, kind-hearted soul he was. Long after his death, I met a porter at some flats where I lived in London, and he told me that he came from Purton, and he remembered "the Captain" who had often instructed him to take coal to old people in the village, but not to tell anyone that "the Captain" had paid for it.

He was much loved in the village, and when he died the wreaths and flowers were arriving all day. In the afternoon there was a faint ring at the doorbell, and the parlourmaid went to receive, she thought, another wreath. She opened the door and on the doorstep stood a hot and dishevelled little girl holding a bunch of wild flowers already beginning to droop in her hot hands, and with tears in her eyes, she handed them to the maid, whispering, "For the Captain," —then she ran away.

CHAPTER FIVE

RECREATIONS AND MISCHIEF

THOUGH strictly brought up, we were nevertheless healthy, lively and, on the whole, a happy family. It is very interesting to contrast the upbringing of the children of the present day with the upbringing of children ninety years ago. I have twelve great-grandchildren and so have opportunities of watching modern ways. The world has changed so completely since those days. My memories of my own childhood lead me to wonder if we did not have a better time. I recollect with great pleasure the fun we had evading our elders and betters. The constant excitement and dare-devilry of doing many things that were strictly forbidden, and many feats that our elders would never have dreamt we would carry out. More freedom than one would have expected from such a strict régime allowed us a more adventurous life than it is possible to allow a child in the present day. The altered conditions make it impossible for children to be allowed to wander about the fields and lanes as we did.

We made our own amusements and I never remember being played with by grown-ups, except at Christmas when they organised and sometimes joined in musical chairs, Sir Roger de Coverley, and hunt-the-slipper.

Our ideas of amusement led to a good deal of mischief. We stole eggs from the hen-house, and potatoes and apples out of the garden, which we cooked at large bonfires which were often burning in the orchard. We consumed these delicacies in "our house", which we made chiefly of odds and ends of wood and faggots. We were allowed to have any eggs which we could find laid by stray hens in hedges or in the shrubbery.

One summer day Sybil, who was much younger than the others and did no lessons in the afternoon, amused herself by stealing enough eggs for the schoolroom party for tea. She came in in triumph, saying she had shut a hen into "our house", and during the afternoon it had laid eight eggs! The result was we all had an egg for tea with the exception of Sybil!

On another occasion Katty and Robert had been collecting apples, and Katty put them under her hat on her head. Just as they began quarrelling, Mother came out and, patting Katty on the back, said "Well, dears, I hope you are being good." Robert, at this moment, pushed Katty's hat with a stick, with the result that all the apples fell at Mother's feet. Mother did not think they were being good.

One of our mischievious practices was tormenting an old gentleman, who, I believe, was a scientist of considerable ability. He was old and retired and did not associate with anyone. He went for a constitutional every day at the same time, crossing the top of the square which was plainly visible from our attic windows. We amused ourselves on sunny days using a looking-glass to flash a light in front of the old man's eyes as he walked along. It worried him terribly and gave us enormous pleasure in watching him. I do not think he ever discovered how it was done.

The same attic window overlooked a rather tumbledown cottage next door. This was occupied by an old man named Theobalds. He was poor with a slattern of a wife and a large family. On washing days we amused ourselves catapulting the washing hanging up in their garden. There were eventually holes which gave the show away and there was a frightful row. Old Theobalds used to chase his children round the garden with a strap using frightful language. I do not think he ever caught them, as he was very lame. This also caused us great amusement. Theobalds said that he was a descendant of the great Theobalds' family. I do not think they had any cause to be proud of him.

Another practical joke was instigated by my brother-in-law, Percy Leigh-Pemberton. My father was fond of asparagus and when he went out for a smoke after breakfast would inspect the beds for the first sign of a shoot. He came in one day triumphant. There were two shoots. Percy slipped out and covered them with walnut shells and we all waited at the schoolroom windows to see Father's concern next morning. We afterwards owned up and Father thoroughly enjoyed the joke.

We were very fond of giving nicknames to people. We disliked Uncle John, Mother's brother, as we considered him an awful snob, so we always referred to him as "little Johnny Jones". I think our animosity was caused by the belief that he sent his valet to the shop to change half a sovereign to enable him to tip us. He was very wealthy and we considered that a gold piece each would have been more appropriate.

Father's cousin, Lady Kathleen, annoyed us by asking many inquisitive questions whenever she came over, which we did not want to answer and thought very impertinent. She was named "Kathleen Pokenose". A respectable bachelor clergyman cousin came to stay and, hearing that his Christian name was George, we gathered outside the door of his bedroom early in the morning and sang "Georgie, Porgie, Pudding and Pie, Kissed the girls and made them cry." His nickname, needless to say, was Georgie Porgie!

Sometimes we were told to stay in the garden and not get dirty. That meant keeping out of the pigstyes and poultry yard, etc. We got dirty and to avoid being detected, went into the boot-hole and rubbed the mud off our boots and cleaned them up a bit. Father complained to the groom that his boots were not properly cleaned and shined. The groom replied that he was sorry, but the young ladies would come into the boot-hole and use his shining brushes for putting on the boot polish.

We played about on the pond, especially when tubs were put on it to soak at a certain time of the year. There was a fence across the pond to a bank. We got into the tub, one or two of the children holding the rope which was attached to it, and we pulled ourselves along the fence till we reached the bank, then the rope pulled us across the deepest part of the pond. It was great fun, we thought, but a smart and stupid girl who came in her best clothes to spend the day with us was reluctant to attempt the voyage. She got very wet, dirty and angry and did not approve of us, neither did her parents.

Charlie, home from Eton, laughed at us and said, "That is not what you should do. I will show you." He got across the pond in the usual way, but disdaining the rope proceeded to try and paddle back with two boards for paddles. Naturally he was wrecked half-way across, amid jeers and laughter from his sisters. He got wet through and was very angry.

The attic window opened on to a flat stone ledge with a gutter below, the roof rising from it. We used at night to climb out of Eleanor's bedroom window and run along the parapet.

At the end of the north side there was a deep drop; an addition had caused this, and the roof ran down to the main wall of our side of the house. By letting ourselves down into the dip, we were able to hoist one another up to the window of the big attic where three of us slept. It was a most perilous proceeding, and I often wonder what his feelings would have been if Father had looked up and seen us. We looked down at him smoking his evening pipe after dinner. If he had looked up I think we, or some of us, would have fallen at his feet. However, this never happened, and we thoroughly enjoyed ourselves. We also smoked, when out on the roof, cigarettes stolen from Father's study.

We had few toys and made many of them ourselves. I well remember a large box to which we attached old perambulator wheels, and had immense fun dragging one another about in it.

We made our own dolls-house out of a large tea chest, cutting windows in the side and lining it with paper. The tea chest was divided into rooms with partitions, and had little doors into the rooms. We made most of the furniture; matchboxes made charming little beds, one half for the bed and the other half upright at one end with curtains each side. Reels of cotton covered with bright material made stools. Little dolls with china heads, hands and feet, and bodies of canvas stuffed with bran, cost only a penny or twopence each. They were dressed as parents, children, maids, including of course a baby in a small box made into a basinette.

We bought little fire-places, a kitchen one and several small ones for the living-rooms. The idea of having fires in the fire-places was suggested, and for some reason I do not understand, we elected to try this experiment in bed at night! Eleanor, being the eldest, of course had the kitchen range, the only possible one to accommodate a fire, the dining-room and drawing-room ones were too small. She had taken paper, sticks, a small quantity of coal and a box of matches into bed with her. She proceeded to light a fire. She burnt the blanket and sheets on her bed. Although she quickly extinguished the fire, the scorched remains and several holes told their tale. She had a sound whipping and all the fire-places in the dolls-house were confiscated.

I was sometimes disagreeable to my brothers and sisters. Our dressing-table, according to the fashion of that day, had a muslin skirt round it. Theodora was fooling about one day and put a candle under the table. I told her not to do it and said: "You will set the table on fire and if you do, I won't help you." Sure enough in a few minutes up went the muslin cover in a blaze. She was terrified and shrieked for help. I sat on the bed and laughed at her, not stirring to help. Fortunately, a maid heard her screaming and came in, so all was well.

One night, there was one of the worst thunderstorms ever known in those parts. A great deal of damage was done, many windows broken and trees struck. Annie and Theodora were absolutely terrified, but I lost my temper with them and told them to shut up. I said: "If God means you to die you'll die, so there's no good kicking up all that fuss!"

We had no electric light, only lamps and candles, and the servants used tallow dips. Our allowance of candles in our bedroom was one candle a week, but later, when dressing for a dinner-party or dance we were allowed two candles. We did manage to collect bits of candle-ends now and then and we stuck these on boards for special occasions and also at other times for reading in bed. I read all Harrison Ainsworth (prohibited) in this manner.

My favourite books were Grimm's Fairy Tales, Hans Andersen's Fairy Tales and Charlotte Yonge's books, of which I managed to get a complete set, and Jules Verne's books, which I think came out as serials in *The Boys' Own Paper*, which we took in. I also much enjoyed *Little Women* and *Good Wives* by Louisa M. Alcott. The most exciting books I ever read were *The Opal Ring* and *The Woman in White*, both read as serials in a magazine at Leeds Castle.

Another book which I read over and over again was called *Fairy Know-a-bit,* or *A Nutshell of Knowledge*, by A. L. O. E. It was all about a little boy called Philibert meeting a fairy called Know-a-bit who answered his questions on all sorts of subjects, and told him how things were made or grown, and where they came from.

Hay-making was great fun. There were four or five men with their scythes working together in perfect time. The long-drawn "swish" was a lovely sound. Huge stone jars of beer were always ready under the hedge, and jugs of tea. Several women joined in the hay-making, spreading the hay and when it was dry raking it into lines, after which the men forked the hay along the rows and made it into cocks. These, I am afraid, we often disturbed, to the men's great annoyance.

We were told a dreadful story about haycocks. A party were yachting up the West coast of Scotland, and went ashore on a friend's estate where hay-making was in progress. The children played in the hay, and one little boy whom we knew hid in a haycock. The governess, who was not aware of this, put her fork into the haycock and also into the boy's eye. He was, of course, blind in that eye for the rest of his life.

We went in the cart going to fetch the hay and coming back on top of it—none too safe a performance. We then, if we could, climbed the haystack and slid down. This was not popular with the hay-makers.

Charlie was keen on fishing, and I used to carry his bait-can down to the canal. I was his constant companion, as I was the only other one in the family who really cared for Natural History. We went mothing in the evenings and bird's-nesting by day. I beat the hedges to bring out the moths. One day I watched Charlie climbing a high tree to a crow's nest. To his delight it had a full clutch of eggs. As both hands were needed to get down the tree, he put some of them in his mouth. There came a jerk and the eggs smashed. They were on the point of hatching. What was said by Charlie is better not recorded! He was furious with me for laughing.

Farmers were kind to us. I think I was especially favoured for my love of nature in all its forms. I am afraid I was often guilty of making gaps in hedges and sometimes treading down a fence.

We played many games: marbles, bagatelle, draughts, dominoes, spillikins, backgammon, and card games such as old maid, beggar your neighbour, snap, happy families and whist. Out of doors we played hopscotch, and in the winter we bowled hoops on our walks, the girls using wooden hoops with sticks, and the boys using iron hoops, which they trundled along with an iron hook. Another favourite winter game was battledore and shuttlecock. We made our own toboggans, skated, snowballed and made snowmen. The snowmen had heads of turnips, hollowed out to contain a nightlight.

We did quite a lot of fretwork, and we eventually had a treadle fret-saw. We made curious frames and brackets, which were given as presents.

We had stilts, some very high ones. One great amusement was to get into an empty house which Father owned next door. We used to see how fast we could get up and down the stairs on stilts. We entered the house through the kitchen window, which was left unlatched.

We had our small gardens, not a great attraction, though we grew our own radishes.

Later on we played a great deal of tennis. There were many tennis parties, some of them as much as nine miles away from home. We drove quite happily to these in a one-horse wagonette along dusty roads. We also started a tennis club in the neighbouring village, where a house had been burnt down and the gardens were let. There we had three or four tennis courts and had many tournaments.

Once a week we hired a room at the Angel Inn to play ping-pong. The landlord's daughter, Ann Greenaway, was a great friend of mine. Sitting in her room one day, I admired an old chest. She said: "Oh, if you like that chest you can have it. I don't want it." It was a beautiful chest, finely carved and obviously old. I told her I could not possibly accept it as I was sure it was valuable. She said: "Well, if you won't accept it, Miss, give me 10/- and I will have it sent down to you." I agreed to this and the chest became mine. I always rather regret that in a weak moment I gave it to Eleanor. It was Tudor period and at a sale of her things when she died it fetched £70.

I had a great flair for old things and, whether due to my psychic powers or not I do not know, I certainly got some

wonderful bargains, amongst others a set of six plain and
two arm dining-room chairs which proved to be Chippen-
dale. I got these for £5 which my husband had given me to
spend on anything I might fancy for our home. At a later
period, when I sold them, they fetched £100 at Sotheby's.
I also bought a settle for 10/- and later was given £10 for it
by a dealer. Those are just a few of the things. Nowadays I
should probably have become an antique dealer, but in
those days it would have been impossible for a girl to earn
her living in such a way.

Old Mr. Greenaway also drove the village fly. This
always went to fetch visitors from the station and we
generally had one of the family on the watch to see it pass
up at four-thirty to see who had arrived. The fly was old
and shaky, so was the horse, and it went at a snail's pace,
so we nicknamed the old man "Tearaway".

When I was in my teens it was a great time among the
young people for practical joking—not always in the best
taste, and in fact, I must say I have an intense dislike of all
practical jokes.

I remember an occasion when, in a large house not far
from us in Wiltshire, there was a big house-party for a hunt
ball. In the horse-drawn omnibus taking the party to the
ball, some young spark thought it funny to light a candle
and drop wax all down a man's suit. The result in this case
was that the man stopped the omnibus, walked back
through the snow, packed his things and left early the
following morning, never to return.

Another joke at a large country house happened in the
smoking-room. It was the habit of the men in those days,
when the ladies had gone to bed, to slip off their tails and
get into smoking-jackets and stay up for some time, talking
and drinking. One young man of the party did not change
his coat, and the party set on him and cut his "tails" off.
The unfortunate young man was not at all well off and had
no smoking-jacket to change into.

Booby traps were also extremely unpleasant. They consisted of something being put on the top of the door, which was closed as near as possible. Anyone opening the door got the "booby" on their head. This was sometimes in the form of liquid, which ruined a person's hair and often their dress.

CHAPTER SIX

HOLIDAYS

WE went to the seaside once a year. Barmouth and Seaton are two resorts which I recollect. We always had a carriage reserved for us on the train, but Mother, I think wisely, went in a different carriage, first class. She also stayed in different lodgings.

At Barmouth, which I remember well, we picked up pebbles of a certain sort called Moss Agates. We took them to a shop where they were cut and polished and made into very pretty bracelets and brooches. We walked up to the Dolgelly Falls and visited Harlech Castle.

At Seaton I was nearly drowned. The governess had taken me out with her and we got into a current and were nearly carried out to sea, but some fishermen came to the rescue. I fancy we were in considerable danger.

We occasionally stayed with our maternal grandmother in Monmouthshire. She was a stately old lady and we were afraid of her. I do not think we were at all popular with her. On one visit we had whooping cough and, being left alone in the bedroom which three of us occupied, with its three single beds, we amused ourselves by jumping from one bed to the other—with the result that we broke two of them!

Grandmother occasionally took us with her on her daily drive. She objected to our country boots and took me to Monmouth to buy some button boots. They were made of kid. I had not said that I had chilblains, and by the time we reached home I was in such agonies that I had to be lifted

from the carriage and taken to the nursery, where I promptly
fainted when they took off my boots.

We had some nice holidays in the Isle of Wight, staying
with Father's old aunt in the little house which he lent to
her.

Grandfather owned some property on the Isle of Wight
which included Arreton Manor, an old house let for several
generations to a family called Roche, who farmed the land.
When I was small I was taken over there to tea. Queen
Victoria used to visit there when she stayed at Osborne,
and I was lifted into a very fine old chair so that I might sit
in it because it was the chair Queen Victoria always used
when there.

On one occasion when I was older, I went with Father
and younger sisters to stay in the little house which we
used after the aunt had died, and from there we went to
Cowes for the day to see the Regatta. When crossing on
the boat from Southampton to Ryde, an old gentleman who
had been watching me for some time, as I was keeping
watch on the younger sisters, came across and offered me
his gold-mounted stick to help me to keep them in order!
He was Admiral Keppel. We were introduced to many of
Father's old shipmates, including Admiral Commeral and
also Lord St. Germans, who was Father's cousin.

Otherwise we did not go away from home except to
Leeds Castle, where we had a lovely time. We went by the
Great Western Railway as far as Reading, where we
changed, having to cross the road to the other station to
the London, Chatham and Dover Railway, where a train
was kept waiting for us. The steam was up, and the guard
with his whistle in his mouth had to run across and bundle
us into the first carriage we came to. This took long enough
for the luggage to be got across. The train was notoriously
slow, and it was always supposed you could get out and
pick flowers if you wanted to!

A carriage and pair met us at Maidstone Station and we
drove out to Leeds Castle. I always looked forward to

hearing the clamping of the horses' hoofs in the cobbled entrance, over the drawbridge and through the arch past the Jacobean stables and up to the front door of the Castle. At this time there were two magnificent cedars in the park, which were later broken down in a snowstorm. From the front door you entered a small hall, which opened into a large inner hall. There were various stuffed animals, including a large pike, 32 lbs, with a carp in its mouth. It had been found drowned, choked by the carp.

My Uncle Philip, Philip Wykeham-Martin, father's eldest brother, was then the owner. He was fond of us, and on one occasion came into the schoolroom to tell us the ice on the moat was safe to skate on, and that we were to have holidays as long as it lasted safe. It lasted six weeks! It was a glorious place for skating and was always kept well swept of snow.

At appropriate times we fished in the moat, instructed in the art by the head gamekeeper, who always had a worm or two in his mouth; he bit bits off for bait. We caught perch and roach, not very large, their numbers no doubt being kept down by the large pike. My brother-in-law, Percy Leigh Pemberton, at a later date caught a pike weighing 19 lbs out of one of the windows. Eleanor and I had to run round to the boat-house to get the boat out. We eventually succeeded in gaffing it—rather a messy business.

We used to play at ghosts there, and on one occasion nearly frightened a housemaid out of her wits. We dressed up a statue in a sheet. It stood in front of a large window at the end of a very long passage, and there were no curtains. It was a moonlight night, and the figure, swathed in the sheet with arms and legs showing black against the light, really did make a terrifying object. As the maid had violent hysterics, we were in disgrace for some time.

On another occasion, our nurserymaid had the fright of her life. One evening she went to the day nursery and, as was customary, knocked at the door.

"Come in," she heard. She opened the door, went in,

and was accosted with, "What do you want?" She looked round for the nurse—but there was no one in the room.

She fled, screaming with fright, and the nurse came out of the night nursery to see what was the matter. The girl told her of the mysterious voice, and the nurse at once realised that it was that of the parrot, which had been brought in that afternoon to amuse the children.

The Castle was for some considerable time the Dower House of the Queens of England. Ann Boleyn and Anne of Cleves stayed there and left some of their belongings at the Castle. Ann Boleyn's diary was in a small casket with rings, to which was attached a cord to enable it to be hung from the waist. There was also a pair of silver-backed hairbrushes, which were supposed to have belonged to Ann of Cleves.

There were all sorts of stories, such as of Ann Boleyn having been seen walking with her head under her arm. She was also reported to have been seen walking from Hollingbourne (where there was a house that belonged to the owner of the Castle) to the Castle, on a certain night of the year.

There were some interesting superstitions connected with our family. One of these was that if a hawk was brought into the Castle, the death of the owner would follow. How often this occurred I do not know, but it certainly happened before the death of my Uncle.

Gamekeepers were forbidden to bring a hawk into the Castle, but one day a new under-gamekeeper, who had not received any order about it, brought a hawk into the gun-room. The occurrence was hushed up, and not allowed to reach the ears of my Uncle. At that time, he had a large party of men friends, members of Parliament, staying with him. They were dining in the large dining-room which was in the New Castle. There had originally been a drawbridge between the two buildings, but during restoration and rebuilding carried out by my great-grandfather and grandfather, a permanent way had been constructed which formed a passage between the two.

The kitchens were in the Old Castle, and the food was brought to the dining-room on heated trolleys along this passage. Half-way through dinner on the night in question, there was suddenly a terrific crash as of broken glass, heard by everyone present. Everyone at once jumped to the conclusion that there had been an accident to the dinner-wagons on the way up the passage. On enquiry it was found that not a glass had been broken and there was no accounting for the noise.

The next day Uncle returned to his parliamentary duties, and within a few days was taken ill in the House, and died in the Library of the House of Commons.

A curious thing happened to my Great-Uncle in another room, called Henry VIII's room, which was upstairs in the Old Castle. He was lying, half asleep, on the wide window-sill. A sudden feeling of fear impelled him to get up hurriedly and move back into the room. He had only just stepped away from the window-sill, when the whole window-frame and seat fell into the moat below. Had he remained sitting there, he would have been drowned.

My cousin sold the Castle some years ago to Lady Baillie, who has altered the interior, and built another storey on top of the Old Castle, which fortunately does not show. I think all the valuable and historic relics have now been given or lent to the Maidstone Museum.

CHAPTER SEVEN

TREATS AND PRESENTS

WE did not have many treats. One really big one once a year was an expedition to Savernake Forest, about sixteen miles from us. We had a large brake which was drawn by three horses; the front horse was ridden by a postillion in a red jacket. I was always tremendously excited about the postillion, and I think it was really what I enjoyed most.

We went one year to Cirencester Park where there was a Fête, and Blondin the great tight-rope walker was there. I was both fascinated and terrified watching him. He had a pole in his hands, and in the course of his performance he wheeled a wheelbarrow, with a man in it, across the wire. He occasionally pretended to slip. His great feat, of course, was crossing the Niagara Falls. He retired, but when he lost all his money he began to perform again. He died in his bed at a ripe old age.

There was a Fair at Purton once a year which we were allowed to go to, and loved. We went on the roundabout, and bought a fairing. I remember a bright blue glass vase with gaudy flowers on it. I thought it very beautiful and treasured it for a long time, in fact until it was broken.

At Christmas one of the minor treats was a Christmas tree for the village schoolchildren in the school, for which we made many things. There was a Flower Show in the summer, combined with the children's school treat. These school treats were much enjoyed, with sack races and sports of all sorts. At the end of a happy day each child had a penny and a bun. Now the children go to London to see the sights, and sometimes fly abroad. What a change!

We occasionally had picnics, generally to an old Roman Camp about two miles from us. We walked there, often on a blazing hot afternoon, carrying the food, mugs, and, most important of all, the kettle. We called at a farmhouse near the camp for water, and then collected sticks and made a fire to boil the kettle.

One curious thing I remember. The stones about the camp were very light and porous, rather like pumice stones. The governess said they were like that because there had been battles there, and the blood shed had affected the stones in this way. We, of course, believed it; I wonder, did she?

There were several parties at Christmas; one we looked forward to was at an old Abbey, Blunsdon, where they had an enormous Christmas tree. In those days Christmas trees were decorated with little wax candles, held on the tree by bright metal clips. A stick with a sponge at the end of it and a basin of water were kept handy for putting out small fires occasioned by the candles.

I was fond of dolls and I had a most lovely doll given to me from the Christmas tree. I was not allowed to play with this except on special occasions and for some unknown reason it was always kept in the cupboard in the pantry. Charlie and my cousin Stanley who were interested in history, and especially in the story of Mary Queen of Scots, took the doll out of the cupboard. Pretending that she was Mary Queen of Scots, they solemnly cut off her head. It was a long time before I got over my grief at this brutal act.

We would visit on occasions the Old Abbey, Blunsdon, and talking of Blunsdon reminds me of a story. Our neighbours at Purton House had a very amusing and rather a larky son. He had been asked to dine and stay the night at Blunsdon, where they were having a large party. He (as was his wont) arrived late and hurried up to his bedroom.

He dressed hurriedly and fixed a smart buttonhole provided for him and, all ready, left his room. The Abbey was of course very old, and the geography, if you were not acquainted with it, rather bewildering. Elton started down a corridor and saw a maid approaching him. He at once asked her the way to the staircase, but, almost before he spoke, looking horrified she screamed and rushed away, banging a door behind her. He suddenly realised he had omitted to put on his trousers!

His accounts of his efforts to find his room again and eventually get downstairs, where dinner had already begun, were funny. They were an eccentric family. On another occasion his younger brother, who was absent-minded, went upstairs to dress for a dinner-party. He could not remember what he had come up for, and so went to bed. The guests having arrived, his mother sent the butler up to tell him to come down. He found him asleep.

Another treat at a later date was the Vale of White Horse Hunt Point-to-Point races, where one met many friends and had a picnic luncheon. There was also Cirencester Hunt Ball every year, which we drove to in a bus, eleven miles, and got back in the early morning, sometimes seeing the factory men catch the six o'clock train.

When we were young we enjoyed Election times. The days of Gladstone versus Salisbury! Mother had pretty little Welsh cloaks made for us; the three red-haired girls wore blue ones, and the three dark-haired ones wore red, and we all wore blue rosettes. Whenever we went out in the village at those times, we were lustily cheered by one party and hissed by the other, which we thought great fun.

A Conservative had little chance of success. Mr. Story-Maskelyne was the Liberal member for Cricklade from 1880 to 1885 and, when the constituencies were altered, for North Wilts from 1885 to 1892. One of his ancestors, Nevil Maskelyne, was Member of Parliament for Cricklade in 1623, at the age of twelve! The Story-Maskelyne family had owned property in North Wilts for many generations, a great deal of it in and around Purton. In Purton church there are several memorial tablets to their ancestors, including one to the Reverend Nevil Maskelyne, who was Astronomer Royal for forty-six years and died in 1811. This was on the wall opposite where we sat in church. When we knew them, their estates had been reduced to a property called Basset Down and another place called Salthrop House in Wroughton. Mr. Story-Maskelyne had no son and the property eventually went to his second daughter, Mary, who married Hugh Oakeley Arnold-Forster, a grandson of Dr. Arnold of Rugby. The eldest daughter did not marry, and the youngest daughter married Sir Arthur Rucker, the scientist, and Principal of London University.

The meetings in those days were often riotous and on one occasion at Swindon, where the Conservative candidate was holding a meeting, the audience became menacing, so much so that all the important people on the platform, including the candidate, left by a side door, leaving Father alone. He was very popular, in spite of being a staunch Conservative, and in a few minutes had the audience roaring with laughter, and they departed quite quietly. On the way home, however, they passed a butcher's shop which had lately been blue-washed. This was too much. They broke every window in the house, until the unfortunate owner put his head out of the window and yelled out, "But I be a yaller!" Poor man, forgetting the coming election, he had painted his house an attractive colour, hoping to get more customers.

At one election a man named Stone was the Conservative candidate and he met with shouts of "He'll sink!" from the audience.

We had few presents. The first of Charlotte M. Yonge's books, *The Daisy Chain*, was given to me by Mother. She had written in it, "Be good sweet maid," etc., and I thought this was wonderful. Another present from Mother was a copy of *Pilgrim's Progress*, which ought to have been a treasured possession. Unfortunately, it gave me no pleasure at all. Although I have tried over and over again, I have never yet managed to read more than the first chapter.

My maternal Grandmother sent a box at Christmas for the children. One time my present was a small black Prayer Book, with a clasp. I was delighted with it and treasured it for many years.

One year my birthday was forgotten, both by me and everyone else, until the middle of the day, then the governess suddenly remembered it and we had a picnic.

CHAPTER EIGHT

FOOD, EXERCISE AND CLOTHING

BABIES were fed on milk and barley water. The bottles had long tubes attached, with a teat at the other end. These tubes were a source of danger if not kept clean. A small brush with a long handle could be pulled through them, and they were always kept in a basin of cold water when not in use. At the age of nine months the first change of diet began, beef tea for the mid-day feed, alternating with a lightly boiled egg and small fingers of bread dipped in it.

Large dry crusts were given to babies to help them to cut their teeth. Bread and milk was gradually substituted for bottles, and bread and butter. The next stage would be fish, probably steamed plaice, and milk puddings.

For the schoolroom breakfast we had bread and milk, with two lumps of sugar in it, and bread and butter. We had a boiled egg on Sunday.

We had milk at eleven o'clock with biscuits, either Osborne or Marie, while grown-ups had a glass of port and biscuits in the drawing-room; men, if they were at home, had whisky and soda in the study, and a cigar. A glass of port was considered good for you, as is shown in the letter which I reproduce, written when I was eight years old.

For luncheon we had mutton broth, followed by Irish stew or cottage pie or similar simple dishes—and on Sunday there was always sirloin of beef. For puddings we had suet roly-poly with jam or currants in it, milk puddings, treacle tart or apple tart. At Leeds Castle there was always a rich

Leeds Castle

October 24th 1846

My dear Mama

We saw the rifle men on

Sunday Uncle Philip took

them to church

Mrs Draffen has taught Dora
and me how to make watch
chains.

Bertha and Corney have
gone to Tunbridge Wells to
see Lucy Draffen.

Eleanor had a sore throat
yesterday but it is much better

today aunt Lizzie gave
her some port wine

Miss Burman wishes to be
remembered to you

Robert declares he will not

go home again
          I remain
      Your affectionate daughter

cake for luncheon as well, but at home we did not aspire to that luxury. The children had draught beer at luncheon, and the grown-ups drank light wine.

Tea consisted of bread and butter, with jam on Sundays, and at bedtime we had a glass of milk and some biscuits. Men did not have tea in the afternoon, but at six o'clock they had a whisky and soda in the study, or sometimes beer.

Children were never asked what they would like to eat. They were given what was considered good for them, and were expected to eat it without comment. I think the grace which we said at the beginning of a meal must have impressed us: "For what we are about to receive, may the Lord make us truly thankful", for we certainly received our food without remark, and, whether we were truly thankful or not, we certainly enjoyed it.

We were called at seven every morning, had cold baths, and were dressed by half-past seven. From half-past seven to eight we were supposed to prepare our lessons for the day, but we generally spent the time playing whist. We had breakfast at eight, after which we did lessons till lunchtime. After luncheon we had to lie down for half an hour, and then in the winter we went for long walks. My amusement was to stop and listen at every telegraph post in the hope of hearing someone sending a telegram!

On these walks we passed one or other of the turnpikes which were used then. It was a nuisance having to stop and pay. There was a most unpleasant old man·at one of them, and a constant threat to the younger children when they were naughty was that they would be given to the old man at the turnpike.

One of the high-lights of our walks was when we saw the stone-breaker. Large heaps of stones, straight from the quarry, were deposited on a verge at the side of the road and men were employed to break these into suitable sizes for mending the roads. Our stone-breaker always gave us a great welcome and allowed us to try our hand. The hammer he used consisted of a stone attached to the end of a short wooden handle. You could beat at the stones with no effect if you did not know the proper method. The stones as I remember were flints, and by holding them in a certain position, according to the strata, quite an ordinary blow could split them easily into the required shape. We would hit the stone as hard as we could with no result, until our friend instructed us in stone-breaking, and this was an art. Under his guidance and holding the stone in a particular way we would hit it, and it would split easily.

It must have been a hard life, sitting alone on that heap of stones all day; no shelter from the weather except a hedge or tree, and he must often have returned home wet through. However, there was a brighter side to it. Everyone who passed stopped to have a chat with him. He acquired a great deal of news and gossip, which he related to his wife on his return home and which made him an interesting and acceptable companion when he went for his drink to the pub in the evening.

One walk always gave us a thrill, and that was past a gallows tree. In old days when it was the custom to hang murderers at the scene of their crime, a farmer coming home from Cricklade on a market day was waylaid, robbed and murdered. The criminal was brought to justice and was hanged on a tree close to the road where the murder took place. An old man in the village remembered the hanging.

Near by this place was a rather dark, unfrequented lane, at the bottom of which were two cottages, one occupied by a really terrifying old woman we called the Witch. In the cottage next to her lived an old man by himself, and he was found brutally murdered. He had savings which he kept in his cottage, and these had been stolen. It was thought the Witch knew who had done it, but the murderer was never traced, although it was considered almost certain that the old man's son had done it. He was on bad terms with his father and was always trying to get money from him. He was a friend of the Witch, and was known to have stayed with her about the time of the murder.

As children we were dressed simply, though we wore an enormous number of garments. A baby was much wrapped up. First, a flannel band wound round the body and sewn into place, then a knitted vest, followed by a long flannel garment with bodice and skirt all in one and fastened with tapes, and a long white petticoat also with bodice and skirt in one; then came a long robe, heavily tucked and often embroidered, the best ones being very beautiful; then probably a matinee jacket, and finally a Shetland shawl which entirely wrapped the child when being taken from room to room. Out of doors, the baby wore a long cloak with a cape, and a close-fitting bonnet much ornamented with tiny ribbons, and fingerless gloves. After this stage they were "short-coated", but this merely meant they wore the same sort of clothes of a shorter length, and boys wore the same frilly embroidered frocks as their sisters.

At schoolroom age we still wore many underclothes—a flannel vest, cotton chemise, a bodice of buckram, on which buttons were sewn for cotton drawers to be buttoned on, a flannel petticoat sewn on to a bodice, and a cotton petticoat with a bodice. We wore cotton dresses in summer and woollen dresses in winter, always with long sleeves. Our Sunday dresses had little ruffles of lace at the neck and wrists, and as soon as we were old enough we had to wash and iron these and sew them in on Saturdays. We wore brown holland overalls over our dresses. For parties we had white piqué dresses with coloured ribbon sashes tied at the back in a big bow, and hair ribbons to match.

Shoes were patent leather with a strap which buttoned round the ankle. Dancing shoes were bronze-coloured kid, thin, with no heels, and elastic round the ankles to keep them on. Outdoor "everyday" boots were laced up and had thick soles, and generally some hobnails in the soles. For best, we had buttoned boots, usually made of kid.

We always wore hats. In summer they were fancy straw with flowers or a ribbon round them. In winter we wore felt hats, tam-o'-shanters or woollen caps. I well remember some pretty white chip straw hats which were new for us to wear on Whit Sunday. On the Saturday morning a letter arrived from my parents at Leeds Castle to say that our step-grandmother had died. Our governesses discussed seriously whether we should be allowed to wear the new hats, but decided that no one in the village would know that we ought to be in mourning, so we were allowed to wear them, much to our delight.

CHAPTER NINE

SIMPLE REMEDIES

I HAVE a clear remembrance of an incident one day when I was about eight years old at the time. I was playing in the day nursery with some of my sisters. The nurserymaid was in charge of us as nurse was away for the day. The baby, aged fifteen months, was fretful and crying and the nurserymaid could not pacify her. Getting angry with the child, she shook her and then she opened a large cupboard in the wall and put the child on a shelf and shut the door. Screams went on for a short time, and then silence. The nurserymaid got up and opened the cupboard door to take the child out, when to her horror she found that it was quite stiff and unconscious.

Terrified, she rushed for assistance, sent for the doctor, and I remember him saying, "Put the child in a hot bath," but Father, who had heard the commotion, entered the room at this moment, picked up the child and took her through the kitchen into the scullery where there was an old-fashioned pump. He proceeded to pump icy cold water on her. Immediately she relaxed, and was soon quite normal. This child, Sybil, the youngest of the family, and Robert, next to her in age, were given to convulsions of this sort, but usually a smart smack brought them round.

There was another near tragedy in this room. Several of us were playing in the nursery and Sybil was having her bottle in the basinette. The nurse left the room, and my sister Katty, aged four and an important person in her own estimation, sat down to watch the baby have her bottle.

She thought she was getting it too fast, and tried to tie a knot in the tube, which was the usual method of reducing the flow. This she was unable to do, so a bright idea struck her that a pin put in the hole in the teat would do the trick. The nurse, hearing the baby's cries, hurried back to see what was wrong. She was just in time to prevent Katty putting teat and pin into the baby's mouth.

In the spring every year, a large jar of brimstone (sulphur) and treacle was mixed at the beginning of May, and after breakfast the family were lined up in a row and the nurse administered a spoonful of the medicine in turn, beginning with the youngest who was her favourite, and using the same spoon for all of us. I was very angry at having the dirty spoon.

When we were quite young there was a smallpox epidemic in the village. We were not allowed outside the garden for a long time. There were over twenty cases in the village, and seven deaths. They were terribly afraid of it spreading to the Swindon works. It was known that a girl from the house where the first case occurred had gone to stay in Swindon. Many of the men who worked in the factory lived in Purton. Everyone in Purton and all the men at the Swindon works had to be vaccinated. Dr. Swinhoe said that quite a large proportion of the factory men fainted when they were vaccinated.

The victims of the smallpox were buried at night by the light of lanterns. We were anxious to see a funeral procession, and we used our usual spy-hole out of the attic window until we got so cold that we had to go back to bed. We never saw a procession, I think because they went a different route and not across the Square as we expected.

We were not encouraged to be ill or talk about illness. On one occasion, when I had a troublesome cough, Mother said, "Alice, if you want to make that disgusting noise, leave the room." I once ventured to say I felt ill and might I not play tennis. Father liked to play every evening and I was his favourite partner. "Don't talk nonsense, go and get your racket at once," was her reply.

Gregory powder and Epsom salts were the usual medicines. If we were looking ill we were told our liver was out of order and that we must take a Gregory powder.

On one occasion Robert was told to take a powder by Mother, and he told us he was not going to do it. As we knew there would be a row if he was found out, we tried to persuade him to take it. Katty, who liked to boss everyone, said, "He will take it from me."

We were all sitting at the schoolroom table, and she asked Robert which was his favourite jam. He said strawberry jam. Katty then said she would mix the powder with some strawberry jam, but Robert said, "Don't mix it, give me a spoonful of jam and put the powder on top." Katty, delighted with the success of her plan, did as she was told.

Robert then said, "Don't stare at me. Turn your back."

Katty turned away, and much to our delight we saw Robert blow the powder off, and eat the jam. The next morning Mother said, "That powder did you a lot of good, you look quite well this morning."

Cod liver oil and Parish's chemical food were the tonics, also malt extract. When we had a cold, the remedy was a brown paper plaster smeared with tallow, held in front of the fire and then pressed to our chests and covered with a piece of flannel when we were in bed. I loved this and the smell of the tallow, it was hot and comforting; I always felt the cold. In winter earache was common, and the remedy was an onion boiled until there was a small core, which was put hot in the offending ear. This gave instantaneous relief. Stomach ache, which I think was caused by too many stolen apples, was treated by making one lie on a hard chair, on one's stomach. It was quite effective, though unscientific.

We had the usual infectious diseases, but never a broken bone. How we escaped I cannot imagine, as we were always climbing trees in the daytime and running about on the roof at night. The only break was Charlie's nose, which was broken playing football in the village. For some time afterwards he was able to press his nose against his cheek, which gave him a most horrible appearance.

CHAPTER TEN

INTRODUCTION TO THE OCCULT

THE first inkling I ever had of psychic matters was during my fourth year. After tea in the nursery the children would get down to play, but I remained in my chair watching Howes and the nurserymaid telling their fortunes by their tea cups. This absolutely fascinated me. First the pouring out of the tea, leaving just enough liquid to move the tea-leaves when the cup was turned round three times. It was then turned upside down on the saucer, left for two or three tense moments, then the cup was carefully turned and the edge wiped free from any moisture which might run back and disturb the pictures. I listened eagerly to their prognostications. I heard of birds, dogs, horses, funerals, weddings, rings, letters, journeys and many other things. I longed for the time when I should be old enough to have a tea cup of my own and see some of these wonderful things.

Further experiences in fortune-telling came in schoolroom days, when Mother, who was very keen on deportment, introduced a backboard. This consisted of a board about eighteen inches wide, on four legs. Two of the legs were a little shorter than the other two, which gave the board a slight slope. There was a hole at the top for the head, and a foot-rest at the lower end, adjustable to the length required for each child. We had to lie on this for half an hour every day, and my turn was immediately after luncheon.

The schoolroom was a large room, the backboard was at the end furthest from the fire, and the two governesses sat by the fire for a short rest before the afternoon walk. They apparently did not think, as they talked in low-pitched voices, that I could hear what they said. They talked about their affairs quite freely, and generally spent some of the time trying to find the meaning of their dreams in a book called, *The Meaning of Your Dreams*, or trying to make out their future in other ways. I was intensely interested and so were the other children, with the result that we read the book on every possible occasion when the governesses were out of the way.

When I was ten I had measles rather badly, the only member of the family to be affected. As I got better and sat up for part of the day, it was a problem to know who to get to sit with me in the afternoon. It could not be anyone who had anything to do with the other children, or anyone who had not had measles. The only suitable one in these respects was the cook, and it was arranged that she should sit with me and amuse me. Her idea of amusing me was to produce a pack of dirty playing-cards and tell fortunes. I was delighted, watched her with great interest, and after a time I suggested I might be able to interpret the cards. She acquiesced, and I told her a lot of things which excited her a great deal.

When I was well I went back to the schoolroom full of fortune-telling, in which my sisters were all very interested. We began trying to tell our fortunes by cards and also by other methods. For several years we dabbled in the various methods of fortune-telling amongst ourselves, sometimes getting good results, sometimes nothing at all.

One means we used was a round wooden table, on which the alphabet was spelled out round the edge. A tumbler, upside down, was put on the table, and two of us put the tips of our fingers on the edge of the glass. The tumbler would then spell out various words and messages in answer to questions. I never really liked this method because I felt that consciously or unconsciously one or other guided the tumbler and often received information according to their wishes.

We were also very keen about ghost stories; in fact, anything uncanny appealed to us. One of our favourite forms of divination was with lead, the process being as follows. A piece of lead was melted in an old saucepan, and then the enquirer poured it into a basin of cold water. The lead formed itself into the most weird shapes, and it took all one's ingenuity to interpret them. Some people seem to have a flair for this sort of thing, and I must own that many of their interpretations are not only full of interest but also prove to be prophetic.

A similar method is used with an egg. You take an egg and separate the white very carefully from the yolk, not a particle of yolk being allowed to mix with the white. Then drop the white into a bowl of water—we generally used a finger-bowl—give the white a gentle stir and breathe on it. The fortune-teller then concentrates on the bowl and sees many pictures in the white of the egg.

When I was about sixteen I went on a visit to Eleanor, soon after her marriage. She was having lessons in Spanish from a Spanish lady, and one morning she said to me, "Alice, the Spanish lady is coming this morning, and she is very keen to have her hand read. Will you do it?"

"Yes, I will have a try," I said. I had sometimes used this method but I knew little of palmistry, just the principle lines of life, heart, fate and head.

I took the woman's palm, and at once said "There has been a terrible tragedy in your life, someone tried to kill you." Almost before I had finished speaking she burst into floods of tears, and I hurriedly left the room, leaving Eleanor to cope with the situation. She told me afterwards that what I had said was true. When the Spanish lady had calmed down, she had told Eleanor that her husband had tried to kill her and had nearly succeeded.

During this visit Eleanor gave me a crystal ball. I was

delighted and found it a wonderful medium. From this time I practically discarded all other methods, such as cards, etc., until a much later date when I found it not necessary to employ even the crystal for receiving impressions of the past or forecasting the future.

Crystal-gazing is an old practice. I have found it interesting and have had good results, and at one time I used it a great deal. The ordinary professional sits, as a rule in a darkened room, with the crystal ball placed on a black velvet cushion or held in a piece of black velvet. The procedure is for the client to take the crystal in her hand and hold it for some time, then she gives it back and the telling begins. I have never adopted this practice. I have always done it in broad daylight—in fact, the more light I could get the better. I merely let the client hold the crystal in his or her hand. When given back to me, I began to see things at once— that is to say, when I could see anything at all, which was by no means a certainty.

It was soon after this visit to Eleanor that I had my first experience of telepathy. I was ill with a bad attack of influenza, ill enough for Miss Iseke to sit up in my room at night.

I was in the room which I used to share with Theodora, who had been promoted to Eleanor's old room across the landing. One night I woke up and heard Eleanor call me as she had often done when she lived at home, but this time I thought from the tone of her voice that she was in danger. I immediately jumped out of bed to go to her, when Miss Iseke, thinking I must be delirious, put me back to bed. I looked at the clock and remarked on the time to Miss Iseke. My anxiety was increased when I remembered Percy and Eleanor were in the South of France. Several days later I heard from Eleanor that they had gone from France to Tangier, and during the voyage they had encountered a bad storm. She had been very frightened and had tried to let me know she was in danger, and she wondered whether her attempt at telepathy had reached me.

The date and time coincided with the time I had heard her voice calling me.

When I was eighteen I had the experience of seeing a living person who was actually elsewhere.

We had family prayers in the morning at nine punctually, and it was one of my duties to open the harmonium and put the hymn books round, and then ring the bell as the clock struck nine.

I was early on this particular morning and, having put everything ready, was leaving the drawing-room. The main staircase of the house came down near the drawing-room door, and half-way up, in full view of that door, four steps led to the schoolroom part of the house. The main staircase went on up to the right to the spare rooms and to Mother's and Father's rooms. As I arrived at the drawing-room door, I saw Miss Iseke coming down the steps from the schoolroom wing. She was wearing a dressing-gown. It was rather a remarkable one, of thick blue cloth with red facings, like a military coat. It was one she often wore. When Mother was not well, Miss Iseke often went to take her her breakfast, so I was not in any way surprised to see her go on up the stairs to Mother's room.

I saw my opportunity of going to the schoolroom in her absence and having some fun with my sisters. I waited until she had time to reach Mother's room; she had obviously not seen me. Then I rushed up the stairs and bounced into the schoolroom where, to my amazement and considerable embarrassment, I saw Miss Iseke sitting at the head of the breakfast table dressed in her ordinary black dress. I muttered an apology and retired as gracefully as I could. All met at family prayers shortly afterwards.

I saw her on another occasion when she passed me as I was going through a swing door into the kitchen. "What did Miss Iseke want in here?" I said to the cook. "She has not been in here, Miss," cook replied. "She is in the garden with your mother."

My interest in psychic matters was intensified when I saw

a ghost in our parish church. The church is very old and a beautiful structure, having the unusual feature of a tower with spire in the middle of the church, which was cruciform, and another tower which contained the bells at the west end of the church.

Purton Church was connected with Malmesbury Abbey, and close to the church was an enormous tithe barn. The ghost I saw was a shadowy form which passed slowly from the south transept to the chancel, where it always disappeared at the same place in the wall in the chancel.

It was not until some time after I had seen this spirit that I heard from the family at the Vicarage that, when the church was being restored in 1872, the workmen came upon a skeleton walled up in a small space in the thickness of the wall. The skeleton was that of a woman, and it was said that some chicken bones were found with it. The skeleton was upright, and by the side was a sword.

In those days, I think people were not so interested in discoveries of this sort as in the present day, and one of the workmen took the sword home with him. It was discovered in his cottage at a much later date by Major Prower, who bought it from the workman, and Major Prower kept it in his house where I remember seeing it. I have heard that it has been returned to the church and has been placed against the wall where the remains were found. This was the place where I always saw the shadowy form of the ghost disappearing.

CHAPTER ELEVEN

HOW DID WE SPEND OUR TIME?

IT is popularly supposed that girls of our generation stayed at home, led idle and useless lives, and that their only occupation was "doing the flowers". This was certainly not so in my family, or among my contemporaries.

Eleanor was a very good pianist, and did beautiful embroidery. She taught regularly in the Sunday School for some years before she married.

Theodora became great friends with Canon and Mrs. Ponsonby, and under their influence became very "High Church", and went regularly into Swindon to attend the services at St. Mark's Church, where the Canon officiated. Mrs. Ponsonby organised classes in church embroidery, which Theodora joined and became very proficient, making altar cloths and church vestments.

Through the Ponsonby's she became acquainted with the Rev. and Mrs. Scott, of Cowley St. John, near Oxford, who needed helpers in their parish. Theodora persuaded our parents to allow her to leave home, and go and live at Cowley St. John, where she did good work in the parish for many years. Father gave her a small allowance, but she managed to have a tiny house, and to keep one servant. She had a natural flair for antiques, and out of her small savings furnished her little house with some valuable pieces.

I took up carving, and I was allowed to use a small room over the stables as a workship. I took over the teaching at the Sunday School when Eleanor married. I kept up my natural history studies, and attended classes in Botany. I studied harmony with another girl, who later went to the London School of Music, where she was very successful.

One winter Eleanor and I attended a course of classes in butter-making. This was organised by a firm in order to advertise their end-over-end churns, which were then the latest labour-saving machines for the purpose. At the end of the course there was an examination. I obtained a first class certificate, and I am sure that Eleanor would also have done so, but unfortunately at the last moment she dropped her butter on the floor!

Annie was an accomplished pianist and a good needle-woman. She had a natural talent for painting, especially flowers, but unfortunately was never encouraged or given any lessons in art. She married young, and spent most of her life abroad.

Katty was a good photographer and won many prizes. She was also a good cook. Sybil, the youngest, also studied music, with a view to a musical career, but did not attain success. She married an organist.

Towards the end of our schoolroom days, education for girls was beginning to change. The era of the governess was coming to an end, and the idea of boarding-school education for girls was becoming more popular. Inspired by women like Florence Nightingale, girls became eager to leave home and take up careers, for which they needed a higher standard of education than could be given at home by one governess teaching all subjects.

Then followed the Women's Suffrage movement, which encouraged the desire for further emancipation. With the First World War came opportunities to leave home and do war work, and once they had broken away there was no going back to the restrictions of parental discipline.

I have often heard people say, "I can't think what those servants found to do in the old days." I think I can show that they were by no means idle.

I am speaking of the ordinary middle-class country house, occupied by the squire or retired service man. Some of these families had lived for generations on their estates, some had smaller houses with no land attached. The usual number of servants was as follows: cook, kitchenmaid (in larger houses there was also a scullerymaid), one or two housemaids, parlourmaid (or possibly butler), nurse and nurserymaid.

Their work began very early in the morning, the younger maids being up punctually at six o'clock. The kitchenmaid cleaned out the grate of the kitchen range, blackleaded it and whitened the hearth, lit the fire and put on the kettles. Once a week she had to clean the flues.

She then cleaned the front door step, whitened it and cleaned the brass handle and knocker on the door. She probably also had to sweep and dust the hall. She then went back to the kitchen to assist the cook with the various breakfasts. For the rest of the day her duties were to make herself generally useful to the cook, preparing vegetables, washing up, polishing the copper pots and pans, and scrubbing the kitchen table which was always kept spotless. The kitchen and scullery floors were often stone, and these had to be scrubbed. She had to lay the table for the servants' meals.

The cook had a cup of tea brought to her in bed, before she got up. She had to cook for a lot of people, because there were large families and a large staff. Home-made bread was customary, and so was butter-making. There was a day for baking cakes and pastry. Different dishes had to be prepared for the meals in dining-room, kitchen, nursery and schoolroom. There were large breakfasts with two or three hot dishes, several courses for luncheon, five courses for dinner in the ordinary way, and seven courses for dinner-parties.

The housemaids cleaned the drawing-room and boudoir and of course in winter lit the fires. The grates were black-leaded and the hearths whitened. Coal-boxes, which had been filled the night before by the groom, were put in their places.

They called the family and guests at eight o'clock, with tea and thin bread and butter. They also emptied the wash-basins, and put a can of hot water in each basin, and two large cans of hot and cold water for the baths, which had been set in place the night before. They then went down to their own breakfast.

After breakfast they went to the bedrooms, opened windows, stripped the beds, emptied the baths, cleaned the wash-hand stands, emptied and refilled the drinking-water bottles and water jugs. Beds were then made, and the rooms swept and dusted. Before sweeping the carpets, they spread damp tea leaves all over to lay the dust. They then swept with a stiff broom, and swept the tea leaves into a dustpan.

The floors were polished by hand with beeswax and turpentine. If bees were kept (as in our case) this polish was made at home. There was a special day for turning out each room.

The servants met for tea at eleven, when they all had a good half-hour's gossip. The housemaids then went back to finish their work, and before luncheon put a can of hot water in each bedroom basin, for people to wash their hands. After their own luncheon, they tidied the bedrooms and emptied the basins. Then there was an interval till tea-time, and if it was not their weekly half-day out they did needlework, usually mending clothes or household linen.

After tea, in the winter, they drew the curtains in the bedrooms and where necessary lit the fires in the bedrooms. They again put out cans of hot water for people to wash their hands before dinner. They put out the clothes which the ladies would wear for dinner.

Later they tidied the bedrooms again, brushed and put away the day clothes, took the dirty shoes and boots down to be cleaned. They turned down the beds, once again put out fresh cans of hot water for washing, filled the hot water bottles, and laid the baths ready for the morning. If they were not required to help with the washing-up, they had a little free time before they went to bed.

The parlourmaid's day started with cleaning the dining-room. Then she took up the gentlemen's clothes, which she had brushed, and their boots. She put out their day clothes ready for them to wear, and took away their evening clothes to be brushed. She then went back to the dining-room, and laid the breakfast and sounded the gong for prayers.

She brought in the hot breakfast dishes, kettle, tea and coffee, and was at hand should the bell ring for further supplies. When the post arrived she brought the letters in on a silver salver, and arranged the daily papers in the study.

She cleared away and washed up the breakfast things, cleaned the silver, and laid the table for luncheon. Before luncheon, she changed out of her print morning dress into her black afternoon uniform dress, with a smart cap and apron. She waited at table for luncheon.

After her own luncheon, she cleared the dining-room table, washed up, and got all the tea things ready for the drawing-room tea. She had to be ready to answer the bell or the front door bell at any moment. Tea was usually at four-thirty; this was an elaborate affair—silver kettle with a little methylated spirit lamp under it, silver teapot, milk and cream jugs and sugar basin, thin bread and butter, brown and white, and several sorts of cakes, supplemented in the winter by dishes of hot scones, buttered toast or crumpets.

After her own tea, she cleared away the drawing-room tea things, and in the winter drew the curtains and made up the fire and, if necessary, refilled the coal-box. She then had plenty to do, washing up, going upstairs to look out the gentlemen's evening clothes, and then laying the table for dinner. At six o'clock she took the brandy, whisky and soda and glasses into the study.

She sounded the dressing gong at seven o'clock, and sounded it again at seven-thirty or eight for dinner. When dinner was ready, she opened the drawing-room door and announced, "Dinner is served."

She waited at the table all through dinner, bringing in and taking out the different courses. After this she cleared away and washed up, carefully counted and put away the table silver, and then her day was done.

The nurserymaid was also up at six o'clock. She did the day nursery and lit the fire. She laid the breakfast table in the nursery, and fetched trays of food from the kitchen. After breakfast she got everything ready for the baby's bath, and did the night nurseries. The rest of the day she assisted the nurse, fetched the nursery meals, and did the baby's washing. The nurse had sole charge of the children, and of training the nurserymaid.

The servants were expected to attend family prayers every morning in the drawing-room before the family breakfast at nine o'clock. They had one half-day out a week, and a half-day out every other Sunday. They all went to church on Sunday morning, except those who had to attend to the hot Sunday luncheon.

They were expected to be in punctually at nine o'clock.

Lamp-cleaning was a skilled business. There were oil lamps for the schoolroom, nursery, staircases and landings, pantry, kitchen and scullery, both halls, dining-room and drawing-room. The maid responsible for each department did her own. The wicks had to be trimmed and the lamps re-filled with paraffin oil every day. Candlesticks, many of them silver, were put on the hall chest and each person took one when they went up to bed. These also needed cleaning every day and the candles renewing. Servants used tallow dips which were bought from the grocer's shop where they hung up in bunches.

Spring-cleaning was an important affair. It took place during May. It was generally arranged for the master of the house to be away, as all men loathe having their study interfered with and know that after spring-cleaning it would take days or weeks before they got their possessions into order.

The first thing to do was to have the sweep, who arrived about 6 a.m. All chimneys were swept, including the kitchen chimney, and the flues thoroughly cleaned. As a rule, there were one or two extra women to help with the cleaning and to do the rough work, especially the scrubbing. Carpets were had up and taken out of doors to be beaten. The heavy winter curtains were taken down, well shaken and brushed, folded up and put away in cupboards or drawers with camphor. Muslin curtains were taken down and washed. If the laundry was done at home, the washer-woman would come for a week, otherwise the things would be sent to the cottager who did the weekly washing.

The pictures were taken down and the glass was cleaned with methylated spirits. Walls were swept thoroughly, ornamental china was washed. All paintwork was washed. The floors were scrubbed before the carpets were put down again. Cupboards were turned out. Every book was shaken and dusted, and the bookshelves cleaned and polished by hand with beeswax. In the kitchen, cupboards were turned out, the shelves washed and everything replaced.

When all was accomplished, the muslin curtains were re-hung, summer curtains substituted for the winter ones. In some cases the cretonnes on the chairs were changed and some of these were washed. Winter blankets were taken off the beds, well shaken and, if necessary, washed. They were folded up and put away with camphor. The furniture was moved away from the walls, and the backs were cleaned.

The housemaids' cupboard was turned out, old rags and dusters were thrown away and new ones given out. Brooms and brushes were looked over and replaced when necessary.

Fireplaces were thoroughly cleaned and polished and one of my great treats was being allowed to go with the housemaid to put ornaments in the fireplaces, which consisted of paper shavings on top of which were placed, in the drawing-room, gold paper leaves and, in the bed-rooms, green paper ones. After this there were no fires until September and the house was sometimes very cold until the warmer days of June. I think you will agree that they had plenty to do.

Service in those days was not looked down upon. In fact the servants at a big house or the parsonage were people of importance in the village. They associated with the farmers and head shopkeepers. The ambition of the village mother was to get her girl into service at a big house, where she was certain of good training and every chance of promotion and a satisfactory career. Those not so fortunate went as general servants to shopkeepers and small farmers and, I am afraid, in many cases had a very hard time.

It seems odd to me that servants, whom we thought so much of and trusted and made friends of, should now be despised. In my day, it was the factory girl and shop girl who were thought inferior.

CHAPTER TWELVE

COMING OUT—ELEANOR'S MARRIAGE

WHEN Eleanor was nearly seventeen, Father decided that the house would not be big enough for entertaining, as the dining-room and drawing-room were small. At this time, Purton House came onto the market. It was a good-sized house in park-like surroundings. The ground in front of the house sloped down to a lake. There had been a dreadful tragedy there. The son of a neighbouring clergyman and a friend had leave to bathe in the lake. They had had a good swim, and had come out of the water when young Saunders, the clergyman's son, said, "I will have one more dive." They were at the deep end, he dived in, and did not reappear. He had become entangled in the weeds, and was drowned.

Whether Father feared that some of his large family might share the same fate I do not know, but he decided against buying Purton House, and decided to build on to our house. He built a wing the whole length of the front of the house, which gave a large dining-room and a big addition to the drawing-room. The dining-room floor was dovetailed oak, so that it could be used as a ballroom. There were large folding doors from this dining-room into the new part of the drawing-room, and the chimney from the new fireplace in the drawing-room was taken up sideways so that the wall above the mantelshelf could be entirely of glass, through which one looked into the conservatory which extended along that side of the house, including the windows of the old drawing-room and the

Father

Presentation to Queen Victoria, 1889

boudoir. The front door was moved to the side, so that it opened into the old dining-room which became the new hall.

The first entertainment given in this new part of the house was a "coming-out" ball in 1882 for Eleanor, on her seventeenth birthday. She was very pretty, with lovely auburn hair, dark brown eyes, beautiful complexion and a good figure. She had many admirers.

The dining-room was lit by an oil lamp suspended from the middle of the ceiling, but Mother invented a delightful way of lighting it when it was used as a ballroom. She had six large half-circle frames of wood made, with holes for eight candles in each. Pink net was nailed across the bottom to stop any candle-grease dripping, and the effect was very pretty.

When we attained the "coming-out" age, at seventeen (or in my case, seventeen and a half), we received an allowance of £25 a year. That was for everything, including stamps and presents. We found the allowance very small. We had to compete with rich cousins, who had at least £100 a year, and when staying with them it was difficult to make a good appearance.

It may be of interest to give a list of expenditure, which shows that even for such a small allowance as we had, one could get a great deal.

1886
Accounts kept of allowance of £25 a year.
Received £6. 5. 0

	£	s.	d.
Ball dress	2	12	6
Blue Print dress	1	9	0
White Satin shoes		6	11
White Kid gloves		6	6
Velvet for hat		1	1½
Ribbon velvet		2	7½
2 doz. Buttons			6

	£	s.	d.
2 yds. of lining			9½
6 yds. of Calico		1	9
2 sets of steels			10
6 yds. of pink print		4	0
4 yds. of check print		5	0
Waist Bands			10
White Straw hat		2	6
Bonnet		5	11
Flowers		5	6
Ribbon velvet		2	2
Ribbon velvet		1	11
Walking shoes		16	6
Total	7	6	10½

We still wore many underclothes—vests, drawers, flannel petticoats, stays which hooked in front and laced at the back. It was the right thing to wear coats and skirts and shirts with ties like men, and sailor straw hats in the mornings. Ball dresses had satin bodices (sometimes laced at the back) and full skirts. This was the age of tight lacing, and our cousin, Chattie Stuart, had a waist unbelievably small, and a large head of dyed golden hair (possibly a wig?). She, I think, suffered in health from the tight lacing. She was very popular, proud of being a Stuart, and possessed many Stuart relics. She imagined herself the image of Mary Queen of Scots, whom she worshipped.

At one time coloured satin shoes and stockings for the evening were the fashion, to match the colours in the dress. We had fans of white ostrich feathers, and I had a lovely eagle feather one, also a Spanish one of yellow and scarlet ribbons intertwined.

We wore bonnets when I was about eighteen, close fitting, as a rule tied under the chin. I had a pretty white one for Ascot of which I was proud, and a white embroidered dress. When I came out, it was the fashion to have sprays of artificial flowers on your ball dress. My court dress had guelder roses on it. I did not have to pay for my court dress out of my allowance.

When Eleanor was eighteen, Mother took her to London for the season. She came home engaged to be married to Percy Leigh-Pemberton, a young solicitor, who during their engagement became a partner in the well-known firm of Meynell and Pemberton. They were married the following Easter when Eleanor was within two months of her nineteenth birthday.

The village was much *en fête* for the wedding, and was decorated by the villagers. My parents were popular and there was immense interest in the event. A large archway of evergreen and artificial flowers was put up over our front gate, and the words "Health and Prosperity" with the monogram P.E. The Workmen's Institute, which was just opposite our house, was decorated with flags. There was another archway on the way to the church, and over the church gateway an archway composed of moss and spring greenery and primroses, with the words: "Long may they live and happy may they be."

On referring to the newspaper cuttings I have of the wedding, I see there were three hundred people in the church, and five hundred outside. On her way from the church to the carriage, Eleanor's pathway was strewn with flowers by six little girls from the national school, dressed in white. The law about marriages had not yet been changed and weddings had to take place in the morning. Eleanor's was at 11 a.m., and was followed by a wedding breakfast. The house was crammed and many guests put up in the village. Mother had a cook from London for a week, and the wedding breakfast was described as sumptuous. A large dinner was given at the Workmen's Institute for the servants and the helpers from the village.

Father was in the habit of going round the house late at night to see that everything was properly locked and bolted. On the day of the wedding he went quite late on his usual rounds. For some unknown and extraordinary reason he was in the habit of taking his unsheathed sword with him and a small lantern. While he was in the scullery he thought he heard a sound in the kitchen, and went back to see what it was. He was just proceeding to thrust his sword under the kitchen table when a movement and a groan or snore prevented him, and he discovered the London cook dead drunk, having fallen partly under the table. The servants disliked her and had left her there, not wanting to take the trouble to drag her upstairs. Our own cook cooked the breakfast on the following morning, and the London cook was sent back to London by an early train.

The interest shown by the villagers in my sister's wedding and their generosity were proof of the regard they had for my parents. I think Purton was a very happy village. We knew one another and took the greatest interest in all that went on, down to the smallest cottage. It is true that the children curtsied in those days, as indeed did some of the women. The men touched their hats, but this did not show any indication of inferiority, merely respect for people who, in their estimation, deserved it.

After this we had a ball every year—each of the girls having a special one for her coming out. They were usually fancy dress. I remember a Mr. Ricardo, who was over 6 ft., came dressed as a baby, in a long robe to his feet and a little frilly bonnet, with a bottle hung round his neck and a rattle in his hand. He was the "belle of the ball"!

I never cared about dancing, partly because I was conscious of being an inferior dancer to my sisters, and my "coming-out" ball caused me misery. I had a white dress as was customary for every girl at her first dance, but it was an old dress made of lace trimmed with bunches of artificial flowers, which had been worn by Eleanor. The flowers were rather dilapidated, and I spent most of the afternoon trying to spread them out and restore them to something like their original state. I had long white kid gloves and carried a fan. We all had little programmes with pencils attached to write the names of our partners. If you were popular your programme would be filled early in the evening.

Although I hated dancing, I much enjoyed "sitting out" with my partner. This was not approved by the chaperones, and I became very skilful at eluding their notice. I never failed to have a partner for supper, because the men liked their food and they liked to find a girl who also appreciated her food and who did not want to hurry back to the ballroom.

Cosmetics were not commonly used by young people, and our parents would have been horrified if they had found we used them. We did know of the existence of rouge and powder and would have very much liked to have had some, but had no opportunity of getting any. To our delight our Miss Iseke told us of a means of heightening our complexion. This was to take a fig leaf, cut it to the size required and press it firmly against your cheek. This had a stinging effect, but a nice rosy colour was obtained. This, of course, did not last very long, and one took the precaution of taking a fig leaf with one, and would retire occasionally to the ladies' cloakroom to see if it was necessary to renew the beauty treatment.

In the year 1885 the popular dances were the waltz, polka, polka-mazurka, quadrille and lancers. At hunt balls the lancers would become very noisy at the wind-up of the dance, when the "view halloo" and huntsman's cries were heard. They were always called Kitchen Lancers. The hunting men wore pink coats, and women had to be careful about the colours of their dresses so that they did not clash with the "pink".

Supper was held in the schoolroom. The older people had a sit-down supper before ours. For the young people it was a buffet supper—chicken in varied disguises, jellies and creams, and on the occasion of my coming-out ball there were oysters. A friend sent Mother a barrel of oysters every year, and they arrived just in time for the ball. Mother was fond of them, and I had already heard them talked about as a great delicacy. At the supper I put one in my mouth and then hurriedly left the room for a nearby lavatory. The oyster did not like me and I did not like the oyster. We parted company and never again did I try to eat one.

Claret and champagne were served, and also soft drinks.

There was a meet of the Vale of White Horse hounds in the village next morning, and I remember getting up before the household were about, and breakfasting from the remains of the supper on the schoolroom table, and following the hounds on foot during the rest of the morning.

Mother made most wonderful orange-brandy and orange-gin, and people on their way to and from meets often came in for a glass. We always looked forward to seeing one old lady, a well-known and eccentric member of the hunt, who had hunted all her life, and who always had a carrot or two for her horse in her boot.

My father used to tell a story of another member of the hunt, a local horse-dealer who had rather a bad fall one day when out hunting. Some of the riders stopped to help him. He was apparently unable to get up, and they tried to pull his arms and legs straight to make him more comfortable. When he kept on shouting, "Barnzo, barnzo!" they renewed their efforts, until finally a local man who knew him well came up and interpreted his cry as, "Born so!" His limbs had been deformed from birth, but apart from this disability he was healthy and active.

Theodora and I did not have a London season, but we went every now and again to London to stay with relations, and it was decided that we should be presented to Queen Victoria. This was in July, 1889. When the time arrived, we went to stay at South Lodge, the London house of my uncle, Lord Llangattock. My aunt, Lady Georgina Llangattock, was to present us.

Our dresses were identical: white satin with a brocade

train attached to the shoulders. The dress and the train were ornamented with guelder roses. The headdress consisted of three ostrich feathers and a veil, which hung down at the back, and there were strict regulations as to the length of the train. When the great day came, our dressmaker dressed us and my aunt's hairdresser came to do our hair and arrange our feathers. We carried bouquets given to us by Uncle John.

We drove to the Palace in a carriage and pair, eventually joining the queue of carriages on Constitution Hill, where we went at a very slow pace. Crowds of people gathered to see the occupants, looking into the carriages and making many remarks, often not at all complimentary!

On arrival we were directed to the Ball Room, where we sat until called. There was quite a long wait until at last our turn came. A gorgeously dressed gentleman adjusted our trains, and we were directed how many curtsies we were to make, in our case eight. The Queen, who was getting old and rather shaky, had just retired two presentations before mine, the Prince of Wales taking her place. This was a bitter disappointment. I was very angry with him as, instead of admiring me, he was turning round, talking and laughing with some of the Court. However, I made my eight curtsies and Aunt Georgie, who was watching from the other end of the room, said I had done very well.

Queen Victoria did not provide any refreshment, not even a cup of tea. When we came out of the Throne Room, we went round to the entrance where the carriages passed slowly, the name of the owner being called. If you were there when your name was called you got in and drove off; if not, the carriage rejoined the queue and took some time to come round again. At last we drove off. On our way home we went to the photographer and had our photographs taken. At South Lodge there was a large reception, and a good many other people in their Court dress.

Later, after my marriage, I was presented to King

Edward VII, which was a very different affair. Things were far less conventional and I remember that I had only two curtsies to make to the King and Queen. It took place in the evening and, after we had paid our homage, we were entertained to a buffet supper, where we met many friends and had a jolly time.

At parties of young people at the time when I came out, "willing" was a fashionable pastime. I was staying with my future sister-in-law, and they had a big party for young people. It was suggested that we should do some "willing". We proceeded as follows: one of the party who volunteered to be willed left the room, the others decided what he should be willed to do when he returned and one of the party volunteered to will him, and he was then called in. All the others concentrated on the action to be performed.

The willer then took hold of the wrists of the person to be willed. Some people preferred to put their hands on his shoulders. I clasped the person's wrists, and on the occasion I am about to describe, I was the willer. Mr. Lambert came back into the room and I took his wrists. They were so big I could hardly get my fingers round them. I proceeded to will him to kiss the hand of a girl called Isabel, and he performed the action successfully. I then dropped his wrists, expecting the usual result, that he would be quite normal.

But this was not the case. He stumbled about and had to be guided to a chair. He did not seem to know what he was doing and was only semi-conscious. We were alarmed and did not know in the least what to do, when gradually he showed signs of returning to consciousness. He seemed dazed but more or less all right, and remained quiet for the rest of the evening.

He was much in love with Isabel Blomfield, and her elder sister, Dorothy, gave me a tremendous dressing-down, told me I was tampering with something dangerous, and begged me never to do it again. As a matter of fact, I never did.

Dorothy Blomfield was engaged to be married, and she wrote the hymn, "O, Perfect Love, all human thought transcending", for her wedding, but her fiancé died before their marriage took place. Later she married a clergyman named Mr. Gurney.

We paid many visits to country houses, for dances and cricket matches. On one occasion I arrived to stay at Lynton, the home of my cousin Stanley Cornwallis, when a Parliamentary election campaign was going on and Stanley was the Tory candidate. He had been driving in his coach round the constituency and stopped at the station to pick me up. I emerged from the train clothed in a bright blue print dress. Stanley was horrified because in that constituency blue was (to my surprise) the Radical colour. I was bundled into the back of the coach and wrapped up in a horse-cloth. This was not a pleasant introduction for a shy girl into a party of sophisticated young people whom she had never met before. They all knew each other, were very lively, and full of jokes about one another which I did not understand. In consequence, during a lull in the conversation at breakfast next morning, I made some remark to the man sitting next to me, addressing him as "Mr. Bishop" as I had heard them call him "Bishop". This caused roars of laughter all round the table, much to my confusion. I then discovered that he was M. C. Kemp, the well-known Kent cricketer whose nickname was "Bishop". I did not enjoy that visit and I think it was the reason for my never really wanting to go to Lynton.

Stanley always had a cricket week at Lynton every summer. He put up the team, and a corresponding number of young girls, and gave a big ball. During the week in which the Eton and Harrow match took place he gave a dinner at his London house to a lot of cricketers and young girls, to which I was once invited. After the dinner we were paired off to go on to a ball in hansom cabs. I did not know the man allocated to me, but he was nice-looking and I expected a pleasant drive. I did not care much about cricket, nor know much about it, but I thought I had better make an effort to talk cricket. The day before I had been present at a match where Wiltshire was beaten. Being a Wiltshire "Moonraker" (having been born and bred in that county) I thought I should be safe in any remarks I made about the Wiltshire team.

"I come from Wiltshire," I said, "and I was ashamed of my county yesterday. I thought Wiltshire played disgracefully and thoroughly deserved the jolly good beating they got. Don't you think so?" There was a pause, and then my companion said very quietly, "They were unfortunate, and had very bad luck. I am their captain." Complete silence reigned until we reached our destination. My escort did not ask me to dance at the ball.

When Stanley came to London for the Eton and Harrow match, he brought his coach which he took to Lords. There were a lot of coaches at Lords in those days. There was a special part, not far from the pavilion, where they stood. They dispensed hospitality all day to their friends— luncheons, teas, drinks, ices and fruit. The Eton and Harrow cricket match was a great event for the boys of both schools, who came to watch and applaud their teams. At the end of the match it was the custom to smash as many of the top-hats of the opposition as they could—an expensive amusement from the parent's point of view, but as most of the fathers were Old Boys I suppose they thought it right to keep up old traditions.

In the winter of 1892, when Eleanor had been married for some years, she and her husband Percy rented a house in Purton, because the lease of the house they had been living in had come to an end, and the new house which they had taken in London would not be available for six months.

In London Eleanor had met a Mrs. Pollock, who had been very interested to learn that Eleanor's maiden name had been Wykeham-Martin. She had told Eleanor that one of the earliest recollections of her childhood when she was living in the Isle of Wight, was of going down to the drawing-room to meet the Member of Parliament, Mr. Charles Wykeham-Martin, our grandfather.

Eleanor had invited Mrs. Pollock's son, Mr. Hugh Pollock, to stay for one of our fancy-dress balls, to which he came dressed as a fencing-master. This was easy for him as his hobby was fencing, so he came in the clothes which he wore for fencing competitions.

A romantically minded friend of mine told me that she was sure that Mr. Pollock had fallen in love with me, and that he had not taken his eyes off me all the evening.

The day after the ball was Sunday, and the party of young people staying in our house joined forces with Eleanor and her party to go for a long walk. Somewhat to my annoyance, my partner for the walk was Mr. Hugh Pollock. I was not in the least interested in him and even found him rather a bore. We got behind the others and were not talking, when quite suddenly I had the most extraordinary feeling: "I shall marry this man some day"—just like that! I was surprised, because I was much interested in another young man at that time.

CHAPTER THIRTEEN

GYPSIES

WE were always interested in the gypsies, whom we often saw in the village. They had a winter encampment on the outskirts of the village in a lovely place far from houses and surrounded with trees. One hard winter when many roads were snowed up with huge drifts, Father became anxious as to whether the gypsies were all right. He got some men and they dug their way to the camp where they found all was well. The gypsies had large fires, no difficulty about wood, and I think they poached a good deal. There were plenty of rabbits about and pheasants. The chief of the camp told Father he had £100 in his caravan. They used a lot of herbs and had stores of flour. But anyhow they were cheery and well and delighted at Father coming to them. He took a good many provisions with him.

The gypsies told him of a remedy for wasp stings. It was to take the stalk of parsley and rub the juice on the place of the sting. It was always absolutely successful, and one summer, when I was looking after Eleanor's children, there were a great many deaths from poisonous wasps and I used the parsley juice with great success when the children were stung. But on one occasion when I went out for the day, leaving instructions that the nurse was to use the parsley in the event of a child being stung, I came home to find one of the boys with a frightfully swollen leg. The nurse did not believe in my remedy and had used the old-fashioned blue bag. I am thankful to say the boy did not die.

This nurse had had some hospital training. She was an excellent nurse and usually carried out all instructions, Eleanor's children being very delicate and needing great care. She left to marry and a few years later I went to see her in her own home. I talked to her for some time and admired her baby, which was then about eighteen months old. She said he had had rather a bad attack of croup. Eleanor's children were very subject to this complaint and the nurse had carried out all the most modern remedies for them, so I said to her: "Well, anyhow, you knew what to do for croup, you have had so much experience with the Leigh-Pembertons." She said: "Oh, I did not use those remedies. I remembered what Mother said. Get a dead mouse and hang it round the child's neck and that is what I did and the boy was soon all right."

The gypsies often suggested telling our fortunes, but we dared not let them for fear of Father's disapproval. But one day when he was away, and not returning until late in the evening, Katty came in, in a great state of excitement. She had met and talked with a gypsy and had made an appointment to meet her at 2.30 in the afternoon behind a haystack in a field down the Sailors Lane, which ran along the edge of our property to the level crossing, where an old sailor man lived in a hut by the side of the railway and attended to the gates. We often went to see him. He was very keen on crime and his hut was covered with pictures of criminals and extracts from newspapers about their crimes.

He often boasted to us that the notorious Charles Peace (who was hanged for the murder of Arthur Dyson in 1879) had arrived in the dead of one night and had had a rest and some food before he departed again in the early dawn. He told us that Peace had an extraordinary way of contorting his face so as to render himself quite unrecognisable and in this way had several times escaped detection.

I have often thought how disappointed the old sailor would have been if he could have known that he missed a great tragedy which occurred after his death in a farmhouse situated just behind his hut. It was occupied by a farmer, his mother and sister. They were all found dead one morning, the farmer having shot his mother and sister and then committed suicide. The source of an epidemic of diphtheria was traced to the same farm, so it was an unlucky place.

As Father was away for the day, we felt pretty safe. At 2.30 p.m. we all six sisters went to the appointed place, including Eleanor who was returning to London the next day to move into their new house in Queens Gate Terrace. We found Gypsy Lee awaiting us. She was a real gypsy, a small woman with a skin looking like parchment, no doubt due to constant exposure to all weathers, jet black hair, quite straight and greasy and piercing dark eyes. She was clothed in several skirts (no doubt with large pockets) and a hat with a draggled feather hanging from it.

I arranged to come last for the telling. She told all my sisters stupid things about journeys, fair men and dark men, and love affairs, but nothing of real interest and then she turned to me.

"Cross my hand with silver, my pretty lady, and I'll tell you a good fortune," she said. I said: "Oh! no, you don't! You have been telling rubbish to these ladies and you don't even know that one of them is married."

She was furious, her eyes flashed and she shook with rage.

"And you think I don't know which is married. This," pointing to Eleanor, "is the married one and she will be dressed in black from head to foot before a fortnight is over."

This was very alarming, but I don't think it worried us much. I was then persuaded to let her tell my fortune. Everything she told me came true. For the next two weeks she constantly met me when I was birds-nesting in the fields, and followed me about telling me other things. I never encouraged her or gave her any money.

At this time I was in love with a young man called Mr. Ernest, and she told me one day:

"You will meet your young man tomorrow, but only for a minute or two."

I was getting bored with her and delighted at being able to prove her wrong I said:

"You are quite wrong. I happen to know he is in Warwickshire and not coming back for some time."

The next day Mother told me I was to escort a lady who would be lunching with us to the 4.30 train. This, of course, I did and saw her into a comfortable corner seat. A few minutes before the train was due to depart a dog-cart raced up to the station and out jumped Mr. Ernest. He got into the carriage and we exchanged only a word or two through the open window. He was returning to Warwickshire, having come home for a day on urgent business.

Sad to relate other things she foretold came true. Just a fortnight after she had said that Eleanor would be dressed in black from head to foot a telegram came from Eleanor asking me to go to her because her eldest son had died. Gypsy Lee had told me the day before the child died that I should get a telegram asking me to go at once (she did not say what for) and that, if I accepted it, it would change my whole life. She begged me not to go. It certainly altered my life. I wonder what would have been the result if I had heeded the "Gypsy's warning"! I went expecting to stay over the funeral, but I stayed four years. I was twenty-four years old by then.

Eleanor was not very strong, having had children and miscarriages in quick succession. She soon came to rely on me for my help in supervising her five children, and eventually her whole household. The children were all delicate, and I often helped to nurse them when they were ill. Mourning was strictly adhered to, and it was a sad household for some months.

The next year further grief was caused by the death of the eldest daughter at the age of seven, of whooping cough,

and there ensued a further period of mourning. It was then
thought advisible for the other children to get away from
London fogs, so a house was rented for six months at
Folkestone. I had charge of the children and their nurse,
Eleanor and Percy only coming down for week-ends.

It was during this time at Folkestone that I met another
Gypsy Lee. I do not know whether there was a close
relationship to my first gypsy friend; Lee is a common
name of a tribe among gypsies.

I had heard a lot of talk of Gypsy Lee of Devil's Dyke,
and, as I was always keen to meet gypsies, I was wondering
how I could go up to the Devil's Dyke and see if I could
get in touch with her. I had a plan, but in those days girls
did not go about alone, and I therefore kept my plan to
myself.

There was, and I expect still is, a little railway up to the
Devil's Dyke, and it was much used by tourists in the
summer. It was a good place for picnics and there was quite
a good restaurant there, also the gypsy was a great attraction.
I told the children's nurse that I would be out for lunch,
and set off one rather cold, blustering day for the Dyke. It
was autumn and I found the little train empty. I was the
only passenger. After rather a beautiful journey through the
hills, I arrived at the Dyke. It was a place like a plateau
high among the hills, quite bare. The restaurant was shut;
there were a few uncomfortable-looking benches round
the place and on one of these seats I saw an old couple
sitting. I went close up to them, thinking I would speak to
them, and you can imagine my astonishment when I
realised they were Mr. and Mrs. Gladstone. I did not
venture to speak to them, and they got up and went away
in the train that I had come by.

The whole place was desolate to a degree, and I looked in
vain for any sign of a gypsy. I was just beginning to feel
very sorry I had not gone away in the train I had come by
(there was not another for over an hour) when I suddenly
saw the gypsy. She was a tall, good-looking, well-dressed

Gypsy Lee

Alice and Hugh, 1897

woman with black hair and dark eyes. She advanced
towards me and I asked her if she was Gypsy Lee. She
said yes, she was, and she was preparing to leave in her
caravan, which was placed a little way down the hill out of
sight. She said the season was over, and she took her
caravan into the town for the winter, where there was a
place reserved for the gypsy vans.

She then asked me to cross her hand with silver, and
proceeded to tell my fortune. She was nothing like my
former Gypsy Lee, who was so clever. I think she had
really been spoilt. She had acquired fame through telling
the fortune of a girl who became the Duchess of Portland.
The girl was engaged to a man who was related, very
distantly, to the duke, but owing to the death of the heir,
unexpectedly succeeded to the title—and the gypsy became
famous for foretelling this. She told me the Duchess sent
her a silk dress and asked her to the wedding, to which she
went. I had a good deal of conversation with her and
promised to visit her in the town at a later date. She told
me how to find the caravan, in the town.

Some time later I went to her caravan. It was smart,
beautifully painted outside, and inside it was spotless,
with a great deal of brightly polished copper and brass.
She told my fortune by cards and incidentally taught me
many ways of laying them out. She always amused me
every time we started a new method. She gave me the cards
and said, "Tumble up, my dearie, tumble up!" She told
me many little things, but my life at that time was not very
eventful. It was an interesting experience.

She used one method which I had never seen used before,
and which I always call "Gypsy Lee's Star". I was a long
time finding out what process she followed in taking out
the cards. She placed the Court card, representing the
client, on the table and then turned over the cards, picking
one out here and there, as it seemed, at random. She made
me shuffle every time she came to the end of the pack
and the process began again. The cards she took out she

v.y.—8

placed round the Court card in the shape of a star, and when this was completed she told my fortune. I watched very carefully and at last realised that she always took out the card that came after a seven, and if two sevens came together, she took the card after the second seven, and so on.

CHAPTER FOURTEEN

LIVING IN LONDON: MY MARRIAGE

WHEN the children and I returned to London after our six months in Folkestone, Eleanor began to go out into society again and to give parties.

I particularly enjoyed the informal dinner-parties for younger people, after which we all went to Earls Court, where there was a big Fun Fair with every sort of entertainment. The switchback was especially popular. You sat in a sort of toboggan which went fast down an incline and up to the top on the other side. If you were not heavy enough to get the impetus to carry you up to the top, the toboggan slid back again to the bottom, and frequently men's coat tails got caught and were torn off, and on one occasion a floating panel on the back of my evening dress was torn off.

Besides entertainment, various arts and crafts were demonstrated. One which particularly delighted me was a glass-blower, who blew little animals and figures which were for sale.

When I first went to live in London, buses were drawn by horses; there were no official stops—you signalled to the driver when you wanted him to stop, and requested the conductor to put you down near your destination. The top seats were uncovered and I always used them except on wet days. It was a lovely way of seeing London. There were of course many trams, which stopped in the same way as the buses.

London in those days was not the quiet place you may

imagine. In every hall there was a whistle and you whistled for your cab: one for a four-wheeler and two for a hansom. This could be very annoying when there was a party next door or two doors off. Rich people had straw put down in front of their houses when there was serious illness to deaden the sound of horses hooves. There were many noisy barrel-organs, sometimes two or three in a day. They were supposed to go if you requested them to, but unless you gave them a tip they would only go a short distance and begin again, well within earshot. There were Punch and Judy shows which delighted the children; rag-and-bone men with their raucous cries; knife-grinders calling "Any knives to grind"; the people who caned chairs calling out "Chairs to mend"; and there were cries of "Sweet Lavender" in season.

There were many beggars in London, and many street singers. I have heard many beautiful voices. There were crossing-sweepers who, in those days of muddy streets, were a great boon as they kept the roadway clean so that our long skirts did not get soiled with mud when crossing the road. The country roads, were appallingly dusty in summer and equally dirty in the winter. Modern children would hardly understand our dirty boots and shoes and muddy clothes, which often got splashed by passing vehicles. Country lanes were almost impassible in the winter, with deep ruts and pot-holes. I think we have to thank motor-cars for the improvement in roads. In the early days of motoring we were always enveloped in large veils to keep the dust from our face and hair.

Along the Embankment there were drinking fountains with metal cups attached by chains. There were water troughs for horses at intervals, and there is still one to be seen in Wimbledon.

After church on Sunday morning, one attended Church Parade in Hyde Park where, opposite Park Lane, there were rows of chairs. We sat on these and watched the fashionable world go by, and also met many of our friends. On Sunday afternoons Percy had tickets for the Zoological Gardens, which were not then open to the public. On Saturdays we went to watch polo at Hurlingham and occasionally went to Ranelagh.

Bicycling was becoming fashionable for girls of our age, and I bicycled down to Battersea Park before breakfast, where many girls met their young men and had coffee at a coffee stall.

As a family the Leigh-Pembertons were much given to practical jokes and eccentric escapades. Percy's Uncle Loftus was responsible for a particularly foolhardy venture which nearly ended in tragedy.

He was a keen Etonian, and he organised an expedition for an Eton crew to row across the Channel in a rowing-boat. He selected the crew, which consisted of John Philips, Charles Philips, Harold Snagg and Cyril Leigh-Pemberton, all old Etonians and distinguished in Eton rowing feats, and himself.

On 27th August 1897 the crew attempted the crossing in a four-oared coast regatta-built galley 22 ft. long 3 ft. 9 in. wide. The Dover Harbour Master gave permission for the tug *Lady Vita* to escort the rowing-boat, which set off at 7.30 a.m. and went straight out into the Channel. On board the tug, besides the captain and crew, were Eleanor, Percy and myself.

At first all went well, although Captain Brownfield on the tug expressed grave doubts as to the boat being able to reach the French coast. After about a mile out, dense clouds appeared and the sea became rough, and it soon appeared the craft was too fragile for the open sea. But the weather brightened a bit, and after two miles the crew were rowing well and apparently in good spirits, occasionally singing the Eton boating song. In reply to enquiries from Captain Brownfield, they said they had a good deal of water in the bottom of the boat. After this the weather worsened; still the crew continued to row well, with the exception of Loftus, who we saw frequently putting only one hand to his oar and who was in an exhausted state. It became evident that he could not remain in the boat; he was, in fact, very sea-sick.

A signal for help from the boat was immediately answered by a small lifeboat being dropped into the sea from the tug, and proceeding to the boat, which had shipped a lot of water. Loftus, having become quite prostrate, was transferred to the tug. Tom Weekes, an able seaman, was left in the boat to take his place in the crew.

Soon it was evident that they could not reach the French coast. The captain of the tug considered they should stop. The boat was half full of water and the crew was sitting in water; despite constant baling, the boat was seen to be filling and beginning to sink. The captain ordered the lifeboat to be got ready, and it was due to his prompt action that no lives were lost. There was not an instant to spare. The boat sank and all the crew were struggling in the water.

The captain gave the order, "Save Tom first, he is drowning." Weekes had drifted away from the others; by hard rowing they were just able to save him. He was seen to go under once, and it was afterwards discovered he had one of his feet entangled with one of the lines of the boat.

I think it was a foolish, if not wicked, attempt to do an impossible task. Loftus Leigh-Pemberton came in for a good deal of adverse criticism. It was an unpleasant episode (to say the least of it) to witness, and I was very thankful when all was safely over.

For holidays, Eleanor and Percy used to rent a furnished house in the country. In 1897 they took a house at Passenham, in Northamptonshire. It was next door to the Rectory and we made friends with the Rector, the Rev. George Capell, and his family while we were there. One of the daughters, Marie, became engaged to be married, but unfortunately she was not happy in her married life, and after some years of separation the marriage was dissolved. Many years later I was to meet her again, in very interesting circumstances, in the Isle of Wight.

On the same day that Marie became engaged, I became engaged to Hugh Pollock, whom I had met four years before when he came, dressed as a fencing-master, to our fancy-dress ball at Purton, and whom I had met at increasingly frequent intervals while I was living with Eleanor in London.

A few days before he came to stay, Hugh wrote me a letter which left me in no doubt that he would propose to me. In these circumstances Eleanor arranged that I should be alone when he arrived and give him tea. This worked out according to plan. While Hugh was proposing to me, a little mouse ran over the tea-table. At a later date Hugh gave me a beautiful silver mouse, which still decorates my dressing-table.

His mother asked me to go and stay at their country house at Sunningdale, where she welcomed me warmly as her future daughter-in-law. Soon after I arrived, she said to me, "Alice, I think I ought to tell that Mr. Pollock dislikes people using the word 'awful'." Although this was not a word which I normally used, this warning made me nervous, and when I sat next to Hugh's father at dinner, I found myself frequently saying "awful" involuntarily.

At last Hugh's father could stand it no longer, and he said solemnly, "My dear Alice, have you any idea what the word 'awful' means?" "Oh, Mr. Pollock," I said, "I am awfully sorry." This was not conducive to further conversation.

Hugh was a descendant of a well-known legal family, the founder of which was David Pollock of Berwick, who was reputed to have walked from Berwick to London, where he established a saddler's shop in Trafalgar Square. He became saddler to George III and to the Prince Regent, who was afterwards George IV. His fifth son, George, named after George III because he was born on the King's birthday, is chiefly remembered for his exploits in the Afghan War. After his return home, he received the Freedom of the City of London, was made Field Marshal, a Baronet and Constable of the Tower of London. He married Frances Webb Barclay, and they had a large family, many of them eminent in various professions. When the Field Marshal died in 1872, he was given a public funeral and buried in Westminster Abbey. His second son, George David, was a surgeon at St. George's Hospital, and married Marianne Charity Saunders, and Hugh was their third son.

At the time of our engagement, Hugh was a member of the Chancery bar, but did not consider that his income from this was sufficient to enable us to marry. He applied for an appointment in the Land Registry, and was taken on temporarily in 1897, being almost certain of a permanent appointment later on. While we were on our honeymoon, he was appointed as Assistant Registrar, which was a senior appointment on the legal side. The subject was of intense interest to him, and he loved his work.

Our wedding took place at Purton in the summer of 1898. The villagers put up arches over our gateway and the entrance to the church. My wedding dress was satin, with a ruched chiffon yoke and sleeves, and a long train of brocade from the shoulders. This was covered with old Limerick lace and a large spray of orange blossom, given to me by the dressmaker. I had a tulle veil kept in place by a small wreath of orange blossom. The wedding was in June, and the reception was held in the garden.

We spent our honeymoon on Dartmoor. This was somewhat of a revelation to me, as I had never been on moorland before and I was enchanted with the tors, the heather and the beauty. I thought then and still think Dartmoor the most beautiful place I have ever seen.

We had glorious weather, very hot and the heather in full bloom. We spent our time walking on the moor, hard going as there were no roads and not even tracks in many places. We visited many of the old prehistoric remains. One day we set out for Cranmere Pool, which was a long way from Chagford and some people had guides to take them there. We found our way fairly easily but were not so fortunate on our return, as we lost our bearings and were getting tired and exhausted when suddenly we arrived at a small cottage.

The door was open and we could see a young woman who had been feeding her baby and was just settling it in its cradle, an obviously home-made affair of wood, not much more than a box. She turned as we knocked, and welcomed us. We explained that we were not sure of our whereabouts, were very tired and in need of a drink. Could she possibly supply us with a cup of tea? She acquiesced readily and placed the kettle on the fire. She seemed glad to see us and chatted away naturally, telling us much of her history.

She told us she came from near Okehampton and her father had taken her one day in to market with him. They had entered into conversation with a man unknown to them. He said he had come in to market to find a wife. He did not know anybody and did not seem to know what to do. "He had a long conversation with my father, and it was eventually suggested that I should be the wife. I was one of a large family and I suppose my father was glad to get rid of one of us." Things were settled up quickly, and she said she went straight out with the man to the cottage on the moor. Whether there was any religious ceremony I do not know. Anyhow, the affair turned out well, and she said that her husband was very nice and that she was happy.

The cottage was miles away from a village and her husband went in once a week for provisions. They had a certain amount of poultry about the place and there was a pig in the kitchen. I do not know what the man's occupation was, but I should imagine that he was a shepherd, or that he looked after the highland cattle of which there was quite a lot at that time on the moor, or he may possibly have had to do with the ponies. They were apt to get into bogs in the fog and had to be rescued.

The cottage was beautifully clean and there was a good peat fire. She apologised for having no milk. They could only get it when they went into a village but she told me that they hoped, in time, to keep a couple of goats. We were much refreshed by the tea, and we gave her something for her pains which she was reluctant to receive, so we put it on the table and left it. We said goodbye and I thanked her for the tea and apologised for causing her quite a lot of trouble. When I said this she looked surprised and, smiling, said, "I don't take trouble, madam."

Later we spent many holidays on Dartmoor with our children, and for several years stayed at a little inn at Postbridge, situated by the river, with a lovely Clapper bridge. Within walking distance was a tin mine still working, and there was an inn called the Warren Inn, half-way between Morwenstowe and Postbridge, where a peat fire had not been let out for a hundred years. I understand it was let out during the First World War.

Many years afterwards, when I was an old woman, I went to stay at Tavistock and, longing to have a look at the moor, I walked up a pathway between some cottages and up a steep hill, at the top of which I found an old man laying a hedge. I entered into conversation with him, complimenting him on his craftsmanship, and then turned to look over the glorious view of Dartmoor. I then turned back to the man and said, "When I was young I walked all over the moor in sunshine and in snow and was even lost in a fog, and I loved it, and still love it very much," and then regretfully, "I can't do that now." He looked rather gravely at me for a moment and then said, "No madam, there are not two mornings to a day."

CHAPTER FIFTEEN

MARRIED LIFE

WE began our married life in the Belgrave Road in a house with five bedrooms, bathroom, double drawing-room, dining-room, study and a small work-room.

Hugh's salary was £750 a year, rising by £25 a year to £1,000. From his mother he received an allowance of £200 a year, which almost exactly paid for the rent, rates and taxes. He paid a life insurance premium of £50 a year. Income Tax was eightpence in the pound.

We kept three servants—cook, parlourmaid and house-maid. The cook began with £20 to £26 a year, the parlour-maid £16 to £18, and the young housemaid £12 to £14 a year. I provided them with afternoon uniform dresses and caps and aprons.

After breakfast Hugh left the house at nine o'clock every morning, and walked to Lincoln's Inn. I superintended the maids' work and ordered meals and then went out to shop, choosing my own meat and vegetables, which were later delivered from the shops. I also did a good deal of needle-work, making curtains and various other household things. I embroidered initials on all my linen.

Being newly married, all our friends called on us and also asked us to dinner-parties. In the afternoons I had to spend a lot of time repaying the calls, and it was also customary to "leave cards" after a dinner-party, and this had to be done within a week after the call or party. If the friends lived near I walked to their house, but if they lived further away and there were a lot of calls to pay, I occasionally hired a brougham in the winter or a victoria in the summer and paid as many calls as I could fit into the afternoon. This cost ten shillings for the afternoon.

If one left cards in person one turned down a corner of the card, but people who kept their own carriage and had a footman used to send the footman round to leave the cards, and then the corner was not turned down. When paying a call it was customary to go in if the hostess was at home, and to stay not more than twenty minutes. When leaving cards one did not go into the house, but left the cards with the parlourmaid at the door. A silver salver was always kept on the hall table and if your hostess was out when you called the butler or parlourmaid would hand you the salver for your card. Letters and papers were also brought in on the salver.

On one occasion I arrived at a house to call on some old friends of Hugh's, whom I knew very slightly. I asked if Mrs. Webb was in and the parlourmaid said she was. I noticed a good deal of luggage in the hall and said perhaps they were going away or seeing off guests and I had better leave cards, but the maid said it was the luggage of a visitor just arrived, and would I please come in. So I was escorted upstairs and announced in the drawing-room. There was quite a number of people in the room but no one I knew. A lady came forward, said "How do you do," and I subsided into a chair.

After a short time I said, "I was told Mrs. Webb was in, but I think I must have misunderstood. Is she out?"

The lady acting as hostess said, "No, she is dead!"

One of the daughters came into the room at this moment, and I fled. It was obviously a funeral party and the lady who greeted me on arrival was the daughter-in-law, hence the maid's reply to my question, was Mrs. Webb in? I think it was the most uncomfortable moment in my life.

In those days the proper observance of mourning was part of the social structure of life and considered absolutely essential. After a death, all the family and near relatives went into black clothes, black crepe being used for deep mourning. How long this period lasted depended on the nearness of the relationship with the deceased person. For a husband, wife or child, a full year was *de rigueur*; for a cousin six months, and so on. Crepe was worn in deep bands on the bottom of the skirt, with collar and cuffs of the same material. Towards the end of the period all except the nearest relatives would be permitted a certain amount of grey, mauve or even white in their clothes. Men wore black crepe bands round their arms and round their hats, and wore black ties.

It was the custom to have a memorial of a relation in the shape of a bracelet, ring or locket, usually with a piece of hair of the deceased in it. Mother had a gold locket with a black enamel face and a diamond in the centre in memory of her father. Inside the locket was, on one side, a portrait of my grandfather and, on the other, a lock of his hair. Jet was much worn, and Mother had some jet beads which I always coveted. Even now I wish I knew where they were and could see them again.

During mourning, handkerchiefs often had very deep black borders, which gave way slowly to narrower black borders as time progressed. Note-paper had deep black edgings. I remember one envelope where there was scarcely room for the address because the black margin was so wide. It was the custom to have your crest stamped on the back of your envelope, and people collected crests in the same way as they collected stamps. This became the custom when the envelopes were made with gummed edges and it was no longer necessary to fasten them with sealing wax impressed with your own seal.

Percy Leigh-Pemberton took us to see a funeral hatchment erected outside a house in Grosvenor Gardens. The armorial bearings painted on it were those of an old peeress who had been a client of his. He explained that it was put up to show that the owner of the house had died, and it would remain up for six months or a year and would then be kept in the parish church until it was required again. It had once been the usual custom to display these hatchments, but I never saw another one and I believe it is seldom, if ever, done now.

When I was newly married it was the fashion to have what were called "At Home" days. You would send invitations to your friends: "At Home—Thursdays in November—from 3–5", or whatever day and month you chose. They were always well attended and quite a good way of seeing one's friends.

One had an elaborate tea in the dining-room of which the guests partook before going up to the drawing-room. I had a Valor Perfection stove in my boudoir and I amused myself by making iced cakes for the "At Home" day. I enjoyed doing it and made some pretty ones.

My son David, when a small boy, showed signs of being hospitable and, if I had him down from the nursery on my "At Home" day, he would make himself agreeable to the guests. He was not more than four or five years old when on one occasion he elected to escort Lady Kekewich, the Judge's wife, downstairs. She was delighted with him, and asked him what he meant to be when he grew up. He immediately answered, "A judge." She never forgot it.

One never knew how many people were coming as it was not necessary to answer invitations, people dropping in when they could. One would have anything from twenty to fifty people. I enjoyed these parties very much.

We also had small tea parties for intimate friends, at which it was rare to see a man, although I had one cousin who went to many tea parties and whistled little tunes. He was very popular.

In the ordinary way we had simple food, but meals were large by modern standards. For breakfast we had coffee, porridge, toast, butter and marmalade (generally home-made), eggs and bacon, sausages or fish. For Sunday lunch we had roast sirloin or round of beef with Yorkshire pudding, rich gravy, green vegetables when in season, followed by apple tart, rolled suet pudding with jam, rhubarb tart or other fruit in season, cheese and biscuits.

For dinner we had three or four courses, generally soup, fish, meat, sweet or savoury. Dessert followed, with fresh fruit and sometimes ices. Ice-cream was made at home in a "Patent Freezer". This was a large round tub into which one put pounded ice mixed with half its weight of freezing salt to the depth of about 1½ inches. The ice-cream mixture was put into a pan which fitted on to a pivot in the centre of the tub, and rested on the ice and freezing salt, then a lid was put on. There was a rotating handle which went through the lid into the ice-cream, and was turned for two or three minutes, before the mixture was left to continue freezing for some hours.

We had no refrigerator, but only a cabinet with a zinc-lined compartment in which was put an enormous block of ice, which kept another compartment cool. In this second compartment we kept the milk and butter, jellies, or anything that needed keeping cool. The block of ice weighed 7 or 14 lb., and was bought from the fishmonger, who delivered it daily or as often as required.

Dinner-parties were much the vogue when we married, and here are a couple of menus of dinners which we gave:

Dîner du 16 mai

___

Consommé à la Rachel

___

Côtelettes de Saumon grillé

___

Mousses de Volaille à l'Indienne

___

Selle d'Agneau

___

Chaudfroid de Cailles au Foie gras

___

Asperges vertes

Bombes Plombière
———
Gâteau Clare
———
Œufs de Pluviers
————————

Dîner du 17 novembre
———
Consommé Printanier
———
Filets de Soles Savoy
———
Ris de Veau aux Tomates
———
Targets d'Agneau
———
Canard sauvage rôti
———
Salade verte
———
Pudding de Noël
———
Paniers d'Orange
———
Laitance de hareng à la diable
————————

Of course, at grander houses there was much more.

At this time Eleanor's cook, Mrs. Allsop, was a great help to me. She gave me a little notebook in which she had written a lot of recipes for dishes which looked smart for a dinner-party, but which were simple enough for my single-handed, rather inexperienced, cook to prepare and were not too expensive for my limited housekeeping allowance of £5 a week.

We entertained a good deal in a small way with dinner-parties for six or eight people and on Sundays we had young men from Hugh's office to lunch or supper. The suppers were informal affairs with only cold food as the maids went out or, at any rate, were free, but we did not clear away or wash up.

At the formal dinner parties everyone wore full evening dress—the men in tail coats, stiff-fronted shirts and white waistcoats. The women wore long gowns, sometimes with short trains. They had white kid gloves up to the elbow and the custom was to pull the glove off the hand and tuck it into the wrist. They carried fans and small bags. I still have a bag which is made of fine petit point and another of silver-gilt chain mesh. In the bag one always had a bottle of smelling salts. These were small glass bottles, with tightly fitting ground-glass stoppers, containing ammonia and scent. Many rooms were badly ventilated and very stuffy and if anyone felt faint a good sniff at the smelling salts was a wonderful restorative. Amongst my wedding presents I had two beautiful silver cases containing smelling salts. One was heavily embossed, about four inches high and three inches round, which was meant to look ornamental on a table in the drawing-room. The other was like a little flask to carry in the evening bag.

We went occasionally to the theatre on birthdays or other anniversaries and then we generally went to the Strand Hotel for supper. I loved these little outings.

We did not stay away much as Hugh could not get away for the week-end until after luncheon on Saturday and had to be back early on Monday morning. Unless it was an attractive invitation it did not seem worth the trouble of packing, let alone the worry of what to take in the way of clothes. If you went prepared for country walks and a quiet evening, you were told on arrival there was a luncheon-party and a dinner-party, neither of which you had anticipated. If you took your best clothes, you went to church on Sunday morning, then went to the stables and walked round the garden till luncheon. In the afternoon you went for a long walk, probably wet and muddy. It was easier to stay at home!

One wet week-end we stayed with friends in a vicarage in Somerset. We sat indoors by the fire all day and were getting rather bored when someone said: "Do tell our fortunes." I, of course, agreed and used cards as a medium. I started by telling for my great friend, but try as I would, I could get nothing for her.

Then her sister Agnes said: "Do something for me." I demurred at trying to tell her anything, as I knew she scoffed at anything of a psychic nature. However, she was very insistent and, after she had shuffled the cards, I spread them out and this is what I told her. "I see a room, a bedroom, shabby and obviously a lodging-house room. The place is dirty and untidy, there is a chest of drawers with several empty whisky bottles on it and on the bed is a figure of a man who has apparently fallen face downwards across the bed. I know he is dead. I see two policemen in the room and there is a man talking to them. His back is turned to me, but I can see that he is well dressed and I feel he is a person of authority. He evidently wishes that the case shall be kept out of the newspapers if possible. There is to be a post mortem and inquest."

Agnes, who had qualified as a nurse, with the idea of helping the sick in their very poor parish, was quite interested and said:

"I am going up for a refresher course soon. I wonder if by any chance I shall manage to be at a post mortem. I have always wanted to be."

About three weeks later the girls' eldest brother was found dead in a room such as I had described. There were many empty bottles and he was found lying face downwards on his bed. It was lucky I did not see the face, because I should have recognised him; or, perhaps if I had, the tragedy might have been prevented. I knew their brother very well indeed. He was an unhappy man. Having tried many ways of earning his living, mostly abroad, he had come home and was leading a lonely life in a bed-sitting room. He was never very strong and he had been ill and life held little prospects for him. He had really drunk himself to death.

The girls' younger brother, a well-known and very successful man (who must have been the man I saw with his back turned to me) was anxious that their name should not appear in the newspapers in connection with this unfortunate affair. I believe he was successful.

Living in London, we were accustomed to watching processions and I had witnessed the Queen's two Jubilees. The streets had been crowded to capacity, the route magnificently decorated, and there were flowers or flags at every window. People had been gaily dressed and carried flags and coloured balloons. The crowds had been full of fun and laughter, and so dense that it had been difficult to get along the pathway. Every little incident had been loudly cheered, even someone who made a dash to cross the road (the police vainly trying to intercept him). Soon came the roar of cheers from the distance proclaiming the approach of the procession, and those cheers continued along the whole of the route.

When the procession had passed the crowd swarmed into the streets and wandered around to see the decorations, and I had been glad of Hugh's protecting arm. Though the people had been good-tempered, it did become almost dangerous, certainly for a woman alone. The crowds had persisted far into the night, when the streets and public buildings had been magnificently illuminated. The thing which had impressed me most was the Cross and Dome of St. Paul's lit up by a searchlight.

But what a contrast I was to witness in 1901! In January of that year came the news of the serious illness of the Queen. There was little hope of her recovery, but in spite of this when I heard, "The Queen is dead," I was momentarily stunned. I slowly realised that a great calamity had befallen England and that things would never be the same again. Then from the distance came silence—cold, impenetrable, profound—the silence of death.

Preparations for the funeral began immediately, and Hugh succeeded in procuring tickets for the roof of St. George's Hospital. This was one of the best vantage points in London for viewing the procession; on the one hand the long stretch of Piccadilly, then below us the turning point at Hyde Park Corner, and again a long view through Hyde Park towards the Marble Arch.

There were still the same dense crowds as before, all down Piccadilly and stretching away into the Park, where the people thronged far back under the trees, but now everyone was dressed in black or dark clothes, and scarcely a sound was heard.

The solemn procession slowly approached, the coffin borne on a gun-carriage drawn by the eight cream-coloured horses that I had last seen used at the Diamond Jubilee; the only difference in their appearance was that their manes were plaited with purple strands. Behind the coffin rode the Prince of Wales, later King Edward VII, accompanied by the Emperor of Germany and the Duke of Connaught and followed by many other royalties.

The sound of the horses' hooves grew fainter and fainter as the procession faded away into Hyde Park, through the lines of loyal subjects who were paying their last act of homage to their beloved Queen. And so she passed to her long rest.

When the procession had passed out of sight the crowds silently dispersed and a new era had begun.

CHAPTER SIXTEEN

THE NEXT GENERATION

THE newspaper boys used to call out the news as they went along the streets, selling the evening papers. It was a very hot summer when our first child David was born in June 1900. With all the windows wide open to get some air, I was trying to sleep when a boy went by crying out "Jack-the-Ripper again! Another 'orrible murder!" Not very restful. There was also a lot of bad news about the war in South Africa at that time.

When one found one was going to have a baby in those days one kept it as quiet as possible for as long as possible and did not tell anyone except close relations. One did not go about saying one was pregnant and using little or no disguise. The word pregnant was not used. One would simply say, "I am going to have a baby", or "I hear that so-and-so is in the family way."

As regards preparation for the birth, there was no idea of exercises or any physical preparation of any sort. One saw a doctor to make sure one was going to have a baby, and, as far as I was concerned I did not see a doctor again till the midwife came to stay and the doctor came chiefly to see her.

The midwife always stayed for a month after the birth of a baby and, consequently, was called the "monthly nurse". There was never any suggestion of going to hospital. The monthly nurse and the family doctor were considered sufficient unless there were serious complications, and then a specialist would be called in. The doctor's fee for the confinement and attendance for the month was £25.

My confinement was a difficult one and I was a long time getting well. I was unable to feed my baby, and will give a short account of bottle-feeding. At one month old, the bottles consisted of:

> 2½ tablespoonfuls of milk
> 2½   „   of barley water
> 1 teaspoonful   of Mellins food
> 1   „   of sugar-of-milk.

He had seven bottles a day at the following times:

> 3 to 4 a.m., 6 to 7 a.m., 9 to 10 a.m., 12 to 1 p.m., 3 to 4 p.m., 6 to 7 p.m., 10 to 11 p.m.

The barley water was made with 1 teaspoonful of Robinson's patent barley mixed with a little cold water. A pint of boiling water was poured on to this and then it was brought to the boil again and stirred over the fire for five minutes.

These quantities were gradually increased up to 9 or 10 tablespoonfuls of milk, and 5 or 7 tablespoonfuls of barley water, at five months, the larger quantities being given in the early and late bottles. The 3 a.m. bottle was then left off. The quantity of Mellins and sugar-of-milk remained the same, but the barley water mixture was increased to 1½ teaspoonfuls to one pint of water.

By nine months, the milk had been increased to 11 tablespoonfuls and the Mellins to 2 teaspoonfuls, while the barley water mixture had been increased to 3 teaspoonfuls to a pint of water. If necessary, one tablespoonful of limewater was given in three of the bottles, but one tablespoonful of barley water was then omitted from those bottles. The midday bottle was left off at nine months and, instead, baby had beef tea and Robbo biscuits or bread-and-milk. Other simple foods such as lightly-boiled egg and steamed fish were gradually introduced, and the bottles were correspondingly reduced. Finally, all bottles were left off at thirteen months. At that age David had cut ten teeth and two more were nearly through.

Medicines used at one month old were:

Magnesia: 1 teaspoonful
Castor oil: ½ small teaspoonful
Peppermint: 1 to 3 drops in a tablespoonful of warm milk
Senna: ½ teaspoonful.

He also had one teaspoonful of Bynin every morning.

There was an open coal fire in the nursery, with a trivet on which stood the saucepan to heat the milk and barley water for the bottles. There was a high fender of wire mesh, with a polished brass rail at the top, surrounding the fireplace. This was useful for airing the babys' clothes as well as preventing the children getting too near the fire.

We furnished the nursery with good plain furniture and the floor was covered with cork linoleum. I made no attempt to get a grand bassinette but bought an untrimmed one and covered it myself with glazed chintz, mainly blue.

My mother made and gave me a complete set of long clothes and short clothes, which she made herself.

The baby, on its first outings, was carried by the monthly nurse, and was always carried for some months before being allowed in a perambulator. The first nurse I engaged for David was smart and well recommended, but rather too superior for my liking. She announced early on that she had a Baronet in her family. She then requested me to knock at the nursery door before I went in. This was too much, and I gave her notice. My relations were angry with me for getting rid of her, as they thought her perfection. I saw a great deal of my children and was constantly in the nursery. My next nurse, Emily, had only been a nursery-maid before coming to me. She stayed for many years until she married.

When our second child was born—this time a girl, whom we called Alison—Hugh's salary had increased, and we decided to move to a larger house. We found a corner house in St. George's Square which suited our requirements, where we lived happily for twelve years.

On the ground floor there was a big hall with the stairs leading up from it and, shut off by a door, another staircase leading down to the basement, which contained a large kitchen, scullery and larder, household storeroom, pantry where all the silver, china and glass were kept and washed up, and a servants' sitting-room. The back door led into an area, from which steps went up to the street. In the area was a large coal cellar which held twenty tons of coal (about 18s. a ton if bought at summer prices) which was a year's supply for the Eagle range in the kitchen, another coal cellar, and several sheds. The coal cellars were filled through a manhole in the pavement above.

Leading out of the hall on one side was a large dining-room and on the other side a room we called the library, and between us we certainly had enough books to justify the name. On the second floor was a double drawing-room, with french windows on to a balcony, and a boudoir. Above that were three floors of bedrooms and nurseries, and one bathroom, which was quite large as it had originally been a small bedroom.

We now had five servants and did more entertaining. We frequently gave dinner-parties for eight or twelve people and I had regular "At Home" days on winter afternoons.

In the library we laid down two tracks of cork matting to make a non-slip surface for fencing. Hugh was a good swordsman and fencer, and in 1897 and 1899 he was third in the Officers' Sabre Competition, and in 1900 he won the Officers' Foils Competition at the Military Tournament, then held at the Agricultural Hall. He belonged to the Inns of Court Volunteers, and at their annual Assault at Arms, gave a display of swordsmanship and fencing, cutting a sheep in half at one blow, cutting feathers and ribbons floating in the air, and on one occasion cut a thick bar of lead in half. One half was kept by the Inns of Court.

Mrs. Gorell-Barnes, the wife of a friend of Hugh's, said when she came to call on me for the first time, "I have heard of the wonderful feats of swordsmanship your husband performs. I hear that he cuts sheep in half. Are they alive when he does it?"

I quickly assured her that they were not!

Unfortunately Hugh developed "fencer's elbow" and could no longer take part in any major competitions, but he enjoyed fencing with friends and did a lot of judging, including the amateur championship, and from 1907 to 1912 at the Royal Naval and Military Tournament. He gave a lecture with demonstrations at Eton with a view to encouraging fencing there. He also took part in Oxford and Cambridge Veterans' matches with the épée.

There were few lady fencers in those days, but there were two sisters who taught fencing and were very good. There was also Miss Toupee Lowther, who was quite a good fencer, but infuriated the men by refusing to acknowledge her hits.

A somewhat strange situation arose over the fencing. I had several relations living in St. George's Square at that time. We were friendly and we often dined with them, and they came to dine with us. Suddenly they ceased to ask us to their house and treated me very coldly when they met me and refused our invitations. I was very astonished at this and remarked on it to Eleanor. She said, "Oh, don't you know why? They know you have fencing matches on Sunday." Unfortunately the clashing of the sabres and foils attracted the attention of children and they clung on to the railings, trying to see what was going on, which gave the show away to people passing by on their way home from church.

Coming back from church with David one Sunday, he remarked to me, "The Maltbys must be awfully rich, Muv." This surprised me, and I said, "I think they are very comfortably off but not rich. Why do you think they are so rich?" "But Muv, Mr. Maltby has the monies bag every Sunday!" Mr. Maltby was a sidesman at our church.

I always found religious education difficult, and on one occasion I had been trying to tell him about the Creation. He was in the back drawing-room playing with a lot of old catalogues I had given him, when he suddenly ran across the room, very excited, with a catalogue in his hand. The picture on it was of an old man, sweeping the carpet with a dustpan and brush, and, on the other side, a smart young man with a vaccum cleaner. He showed these to me with this remark: "Muv, I have found a picture of God sweeping up the dust and here is the picture of the man he has made!"

On another occasion, I was reading to him about Adam and Eve, and how Eve was created from one of Adam's ribs. His remark on this occasion was: "I think that's beastly cruel. I won't listen to it." And he burst into tears and rushed out of the room.

He went to a preparatory school when he was nine. When I took him by train for his first term he had an unfortunate accident. When someone left the carriage, he got up to look out, with his hand on the lintel of the door. A porter, passing by, banged the door shut and David's fingers were caught. He was extraordinarily brave about it, but the Matron at the school was horrified at the appearance of his hand. It was not a bright beginning for his school career. He stayed at this school for two years and then went to Blatchington School at Seaford. He followed his father by going to Harrow and afterwards to Trinity College, Cambridge.

As we lived in London, Alison was able to complete her education at day schools, supplemented by weekly visits to Miss Wordsworth's dancing class in Harrington Gardens. Miss Wordsworth was short and stout, like Queen Victoria in appearance. She was a strict disciplinarian and her stentorian voice terrified her pupils and even their nannies.

When our nannie left and went to Canada, Helen came to us as what was then called a "useful maid". Her duties were to take Alison to and from her first school and for walks in the afternoons—usually to Battersea Park, which was then a quiet, peaceful place. She also looked after my clothes as well as Alison's, did the mending and was, in fact, generally "useful". During the First World War, when the other maids left to do war work, she took on many of their duties, including cooking. She taught Alison the rudiments of cooking on the big coal-fired Eagle range in the kitchen at St. George's Square. Later she also emigrated to Canada to join two of her sisters, who had previously been with us as parlourmaid and housemaid. They still, even today, come to see us whenever they have saved up enough to take a trip back to the "old country".

In 1913 the Oxford and Cambridge Fencing Match was held in London for the first time. Hugh asked the two teams, the judges and a few other fencing friends to dinner, making a party of twenty-four.

I superintended the laying of the table, and arranged the flowers. On this occasion the flowers were light blue and dark blue. Light blue and dark blue ribbons were criss-crossed on the white tablecloth.

The menu cards had a special design of a sabre and a foil printed on top of the card, some in light blue and some in dark blue.

13th May 1913

MENU

Consommé aux Petits Choux

———

Saumon—Sauce Verte

———

Crême de Volaille

———

Selle d'Agneau

———

Salade a l'Imperiale

———

Crême aux Fraises

———

Pouding à la Valentia

———

Délices de Laitance

———————

I give the prices to show what things cost in those days:

	£	s.	d.
Sweets		7	1½
Princess rolls		1	0
Fish and shells for ice		1	10
Vanilla ice-cream		13	0
Quails	1	0	0
French beans		6	0
Terragon and chervil			4
Potatoes		1	0
Spinach		3	0
Cucumbers			6
Lettuces		1	6
Melon		4	0
Pineapple		5	0
Cream		3	9
Truffles		1	9
Herring roes		1	3
Stock meat		2	11½
,, ,,		2	2½
Salmon		16	0
Lamb	1	4	3
Watercress			2
Cream		1	6
Devonshire cream & postage		3	1
Ice		2	3
	6	3	5½

This dinner was cooked by my single-handed cook, her only help being her sister who came in for the evening.

We hired two waiters at £1 each. The party was for men only so I was not present at the dinner. Being anxious to see how things were going, I occasionally looked over the staircase down into the hall. I was most amused to see one waiter helping the other to large spoonfuls of strawberries and cream. I also saw they were drinking a good deal of the champagne, which they opened in the library before serving it in the dining-room.

There was a nice garden at St. George's Square, to which all the residents had keys. It was a delightful place for the children to play.

Canon and Mrs. Thorndyke lived in a house in the Square, and I knew them slightly. Their daughter Sybil used to visit them with her first baby, when it was quite small. On Sunday afternoons (when I suppose her nurse was off duty), Sybil took her baby round the garden in its pram. She was pretty and always beautifully dressed. One summer day, when her dress was of some diaphanous material, she had either forgotten to put on her petticoat, or it was transparent, and her legs were clearly visible as she walked round the garden. We watched her with some amusement, although slightly shocked. Legs were not supposed to be visible in those days.

I think we did more than most people on our income. We were both very keen on sport. Hugh was a good shot and also a good fisherman. When I married I had no experience of fly-fishing and did not even own a rod. Hugh gave me a lovely little rod and my first lessons in fly-fishing were when we were on a holiday on Exmoor, where we stayed at an inn and fished in the river.

After we had been married three years, Hugh had a legacy of £200 left to him by an old aunt, and we decided to take a shoot in Scotland with a friend of Hugh's, Mr. Hulton. The shoot was a place called Lennel at Coldstream. We had good sport and a most enjoyable time. For several of our holidays we took rough shooting, twice on Mull and once at Stratton-on-the-Fosse.

As the children grew older we wanted to include them in our holidays. Sometimes we rented a cottage and once a farmhouse at Morwenstow—where I had occasion to go down in the night to fetch something and saw a large quantity of rats sitting round the fire!

I asked the farmer's wife to give me the names of butcher, baker and other tradesmen. The butcher called once a week from Bude, but when I came to the baker, she said, "No baker calls. You will have to make your own bread." This I did quite successfully with the help of Emily, and we had yeast sent by post.

In 1909 our thoughts turned back to Dartmoor, which is in the parish of Lydford, and to Lydford we went. We rented an unfurnished cottage at Shellaford, on the outskirts of Lydford, for two years and spent our holidays there. This cottage was somewhat primitive. It had one lavatory, and cold water laid on to a sink in the kitchen. This water was not fit for drinking purposes and drinking water had to be fetched from a spring which was a little way down the road.

We got over the difficulty of having no hot water supply by purchasing from the Institute for the Blind at Exeter "cosy-cans". These consisted of large baskets with a thickly padded lining, into which were deposited large zinc cans. We had several of these cans, which were filled with boiling water during the day and provided us and the children with hot baths in the morning. We had small rubber baths which folded up when not in use—and sometimes when in use.

Hugh had a licence for snipe-shooting on the moor. This afforded us a good excuse for spending long days on the moor, where the children enjoyed their freedom and ran wild, fishing in the little streams and picking whortleberries, and riding an old Dartmoor pony.

We had such a happy time there and became so fond of

Lydford that in 1911 we decided to build a house there. We bought two acres of glebe land and built a charming house. At first we only occupied the ground floor, although we put windows and fireplaces in the upper floor, which was approached by a ladder and was kept as an open space. This provided a delightful playroom for the children. One of their amusements was roller-skating.

For several years we had lovely holidays. We made a large garden and kept a pony and governess cart. Natural history was our chief amusement, David being very keen. He has retained his love of nature, especially birds, of which he has a considerable knowledge.

Our idea was that when the time came for Hugh's retirement we should go and live there permanently. In 1914, at the beginning of the Great War, Hugh had a serious illness and was away from work for six months, which we spent at Lydford. This made us realise that it would be too remote for our children when they grew up.

In the early days of the war it was difficult to get transport even in these rather remote regions; many horses had been commandeered for the Army and motor vans were not at all common. We were in urgent need of coal for the kitchen range, on which the cooking was done and which heated the water. We heard that the coal had arrived at the station, but would we please fetch it, as they had no means of sending it. We had a small two-wheeled farm cart (locally called a putt) to which we harnessed our pony. David and Alison, aged 14 and 11, drove down to the station, loaded up and brought the coal back. David drove the pony and Alison sat on the tailboard and read *Pickwick Papers* on the way. It was only two miles to the station, but they had to make a good many trips and they were black from head to foot by the time they had finished.

After the peace of Dartmoor it was rather terrible to come back to London to the many restrictions and to the Zeppelins coming over, occasionally in the daytime but generally in the early evening. St. George's Square was close to the river, and at one time the Zeppelins used to come up the river, always from about seven till eight o'clock in the evening, and turn just before they got to the Square, going over towards Westminster. On many mornings there was a quantity of shrapnel in the area.

Life for the ordinary individual took on an entirely new aspect. We had kept five servants—we were now reduced to one, the reason being that the women went to fill up the men's places in factories, making munitions, in shops, banks and on the land, also gardening; in fact, doing the men's work and doing it well. Many, of course, went to work in hospitals.

Everything in the house was simplified. The drawing-room was shut up and covered with dust sheets. A spare room was always kept ready for anyone who might turn up unexpectedly. Breakfast and luncheon were reduced to one course each, and dinner to two or three. For the first time for as long as I could remember people began to be slack about dressing for dinner. Men often came in from work tired and wanting their meals at once, and, having to wash up, one did not want to be in evening dress. A thick apron was the usual change! Times, also, were very irregular to suit the workers. Also, about this time, people dropped in on their way home from work for a chat and a glass of sherry. This was the beginning of what we now call cocktail parties. When the young people came on leave they amused themselves with thé-dansants. The Piccadilly Hotel was one of the favourite places. You went in and ordered your tea and danced on a small floor around which the tables were arranged.

The first Zeppelin to be brought down in England was the L 33, which was brought down by gunfire at Great Wigborough, Mersea, Essex, on 24th September 1916, $7\frac{1}{2}$ miles from Colchester and $4\frac{1}{2}$ miles from D'Arcy, on the Great Eastern Railway. I went to see this and was given a piece of twisted metal from the Zeppelin, which I still

Family Group, 1897

Back row : Judy (Robert's fiancée), Percy and Eleanor, Charlie and Connie, Hugh and Alice
Second row : Kathy, Robert, Mother, Father, Theodora, Annie and Harry
"Little Charlie" (Charlie's son)
Front row : Perce (Eleanor's son)   Sybil

David and Alison, ready for Church, 1908

have. I also have some of the shrapnel out of our own area in London.

During the following year we took a short holiday in Essex, hoping to get away from the noise. I do not think we quite realised it was not the best place to find quiet. When we arrived at the house we had taken, we found the one that adjoined it had been razed to the ground a short time before by a bomb!

Alison was taken very ill there and, feeling it imperative for her to be taken at once to London by car, I managed with great difficulty to get permission to motor up. We arranged to have a nurse waiting for us and, in time, Alison got over her illness. I had sent Helen, our housekeeper, on by train to prepare a room for the invalid and get in some food. The house was being looked after by a policeman and his wife and was, therefore, in quite good order.

We left David, aged 17, to shut up the house in Essex and, when I asked him how he managed to cook his breakfast, he said, "I didn't. I found a piece of plum-pudding in the larder and I ate that!"

As regards want of servants, it was hard on some of the old people. Their sons had gone to the war, their daughters were doing war work, in all probability away from home, and they were left, sometimes with only one servant and that an old one, possibly a nanny. People of that generation had not been taught to cook and had never fended for themselves at all, and I think great hardships were endured. It is a remarkable thing that with all the troubles and inconveniences I practically never heard anyone grumble.

Some of the old servants were wonderful. I knew of old butlers, on the eve of retiring, turning to single-handed and making a splendid job of it. Elderly cooks, accustomed to kitchenmaids and scullerymaids, managed alone, and I need hardly say that the nannies were always ready to come to the rescue. In fact, everyone did their bit.

PART TWO

Natural and Supernatural

CHAPTER SEVENTEEN

THE CRYSTAL AND PSYCHOMETRY

I HAVE had many psychic experiences during my life. As I said earlier, the interest had been there since I was a small girl. My Mother had a "sixth sense" and was sometimes forewarned of things that were to happen. All my sisters had a certain amount of psychic power, but none of them developed it to the extent that I did. Eleanor was the one who was most interested and encouraged me to use my power; it was she who gave me my first crystal, and she introduced me to people who wanted help either in foreseeing the future or in uncovering the past of a house or property by psychometry. These introductions often led to the most unexpected adventures such as the following.

In November 1910 I received an invitation from Eleanor to stay with her at her house in Kent. It had been foggy and I had had a bad attack of bronchitis, and was delighted at the opportunity of getting out of London to get some fresh country air for a bit.

We had not met for some little time and I was looking forward to cosy talks on many subjects, some important. I left London by an early train and Eleanor met me at Ashford station. I was secretly annoyed when she said, "We are going to have an early lunch, as I am going to take you to a haunted house. I have promised the owners that you will psychometrise the house and see if you can find the cause of the haunting, which is giving them much concern."

She said she had met two middle-aged ladies at a friend's

house and they had told her that they had taken a ninety-nine years lease on an old house and done a good deal in the way of restoration. The house had been unoccupied for some years and had been used by gypsies and vagrants. They said it was a charming house and they were already fond of it, but they were constantly aware of a presence which they could feel, but they had not seen anything, and there were many little things which worried them, but they would not say more. They were very excited when Eleanor told them she had a sister who was psychic, and they implored her to bring me over when I came to stay. Eleanor said she expected me for a few days, and they arranged the afternoon of my arrival as a convenient time for me to go there.

After lunch we started out. It was a dismal afternoon, everything dripping wet, rather foggy and raining every now and then. On our way we nearly had a bad accident. There was a steep hill, called Steed Hill, which we had to negotiate, and when half-way up the hill the car began going backwards. I was alarmed, but the driver managed somehow to prevent it gathering speed and, before the bottom of the hill was reached, we stopped. After this unpleasant experience all went well and we arrived at Yokes Court.

Some rather handsome iron gates stood open, on either side of which were stone pillars. In the fading light I could see that the house was a large building of red brick, but I could see no details of architecture. We entered the gateway and drove down quite a short drive to the side of the house where there was a small modern door in no way imposing. At the door we were greeted by the two elderly ladies and their niece, Miss Tenison.

I was introduced by Eleanor, and I at once said, "My sister tells me you want me to try and psychometrise your house. If so, will you please, without having any conversation with me, let me go straight into the house and go where I like."

They said, "Certainly," and I went forward into the small

hall, or lobby—you could hardly dignify it by the name of hall. There were three doors, one straight in front, one on the left, and one on the right. I chose the left-hand door, which I opened and found myself in a large banqueting hall, sparsely furnished—a long refectory table, a few chairs, the floor covered with matting. This room gave me no feeling at all and I walked across to the further end, where there was a door on the right. This door led into a small hall with a staircase leading to a half-landing, from either side of which stairs led up to the bedroom floor. I turned to my right and opened a door which led me into what was evidently the dining-room. It was a long, rather narrow room with a window at the end. There was a modern fireplace. On the right as I came into the room there was a niche in the thick wall which divided this room from the banqueting hall. This room, I felt, was full of atmosphere, and I put my crystal down on the floor and left it for several minutes.

Before I could pick it up again, the whole scene had changed, and I described what I saw. The wall between the hall and the dining-room disappeared, making one large hall. There was a large old-fashioned open fireplace with logs blazing on the hearth; a small boy was lying in front of the fire playing with some toys. There was a massive door in place of the niche. The door opened and a villainous-looking man entered, dressed in old-fashioned clothes, I should imagine about the Elizabethan period. He wore a hat pulled low over his forehead and stood for a moment looking at the boy.

The boy, disturbed by the creaking of the door, looked up, and when he saw the man he rose, looking terrified, and began moving away. The man stepped forward, and as he did so the boy gave a scream, and the man, raising his arm, hit the boy a frightful blow on the head. I knew at once the boy was dead. As his scream faded, a lovely woman appeared on the stairs. She rushed down and knelt by the side of the boy. I saw the man move to the door, which he had left partly open. He opened it wider and went out. I saw that it was snowing fast outside.

The whole vision then faded, and everything was again normal. I left the room, returning to the small hall, and made for another door which was partly under the stairs. For the first time one of the old ladies spoke, saying, "Be careful—there are stairs there."

Opening the door carefully, I found I was at the top of steps leading down to the cellar. I asked the others to go first. Half-way down the stairs there was a ledge jutting out from the wall, with some large stones.

"There was a skeleton here, but it is not here now," I said, putting my hand on a stone. "Did you find one?"

They looked worried and uncomfortable, and acknowledged that a skeleton had been found there when the workmen were putting in heating apparatus.

"But you didn't find the head, did you?" I said.

No, they had not. Was this the skeleton of the boy I had seen killed? And was the head so crushed that it fell to pieces? We shall never know, but I am sure if I had had my way I could have found the remains of the head, which I felt were nearby.

They now suggested that I needed a rest and we went to the banqueting hall, where we had an extremely good tea, and much interesting conversation about psychic phenomena. Miss Tenison told us she was a firm believer in reincarnation, and that she distinctly remembered the details of her existence in former incarnations. She was sure that she had been Claverhouse; she had also been a Marquis during the French Revolution. I have never been able to believe in re-incarnation, though I am open to conviction. Eleanor was quite sure that she had been an Egyptian princess.

Some weeks later we heard from Miss Tenison that she had asked the architect who had supervised the restoration, where the original front door would have been. He replied that the original front door of the Tudor House was situated where now there was a niche in the dining-room wall, which was originally the outside wall of the house. He also said that the banqueting hall was a fifteenth-century addition. Some of the hauntings continued. They had the house exorcised by a clergyman, but even this did not stop the visitations, especially in one of the bedrooms.

After my first visit to Yokes, I went there on many other occasions. Walking in the garden alone one day, I looked towards the house, when to my amazement I saw a much older house with an outside staircase which led down to a courtyard, full of soldiers in armour. Then I heard a voice calling, "Roger, Roger, Roger," three times. I was certain that Roger was going away and would never come back.

I told Miss Tenison what I had seen, and she was later able to verify the details from old records. She found that a man named Roger had gone to the Crusades from Yokes Court and had not returned.

I soon realised that Miss Tenison was very clever, and that she was idolised by her aunts. She had a sitting-room upstairs, where she spent nearly all her time writing. They were always mysterious about this. She was rather delicate, and her aunts took it in turn to fill hot water bottles for her at frequent intervals, as she felt the cold when she was sitting all day at her desk. They sacrificed everything to her, and they sold some beautiful pictures by Varley to provide money for her to continue the costly research for her great work.

We heard later that this work was: *Elizabethan England: being the History of the Country in relation to all Foreign Princes*, by E. M. Tenison, Officer of the Order of St. John of Jerusalem, Member of the Real Academia de la Historia de Espana, Member of the Society for Nautical Research. Issued to Subscribers only. There were twelve volumes. She was obsessed with the idea that if it was known that it was written by a woman it would not be read even if it was published. Many people she communicated with about the book were convinced that it was written by a man.

She also wrote under the name of Michael Barrington several romances and biographies. One of these was a biography of *Grahame of Claverhouse, Viscount Dundee*, which I presume was founded on her experience in her former incarnation. She also wrote poetry, of which she frequently sent me little booklets. Many of her poems I liked very much.

Elizabethan England was not finished until after the death of both her aunts. When the faithful old maidservant, having continued to look after her for many years, also died, Miss Tenison remained alone, and a terrible misfortune overtook her. She had just completed the twelfth volume, and had it spread out for final corrections, when she was called out of the room by the daily maid, and she left the door open. The window was also open, and the manuscript blew into the fire and soon the whole room was ablaze. Everything in the room was destroyed, including the only copy of the final volume.

A large part of the house was damaged, and she left it and went to live at Headingham in Essex. Although it seems almost incredible, she set to work and rewrote the whole of the twelfth volume without any notes, and it was published not long before her death.

Once, soon after I was married, Eleanor came to see me on her own account, but the result of her enquiry was more than either of us had bargained for.

I was busy sewing one afternoon when the doorbell rang and Eleanor was announced. As usual she was full of life and had much of interest to tell me, but almost at once she said, "I have really come to see if you can get anything in the crystal for me. It is quite likely I will have to go to Spain almost immediately, and I wonder could you see anything about my journey and especially the outcome of it."

Much as I disliked to be asked particular questions about persons or plans or even events, I saw that Eleanor was excited and also worried, and I said I would see what I could do. I held the crystal for a moment or two, then suddenly I saw our Mother, who, as far as I knew, was at home in the country. She was in a small, rather dingy-looking room, seated in a chair. With her was her companion, Miss Iseke, and a strange man. As I looked I saw blood streaming from her nose, and then no more.

We both thought it odd but quite impossible that there should be any truth it it. I could see nothing for Eleanor, and after a time she got up to go. I accompanied her to the front door, and I noticed a letter in the letter-box. Taking it out I saw it was from Mother, and said, "Wait a moment, we will see if there is any news. It is odd a letter from Mother coming by this post. Her letters always arrive either by the morning post or the 8.30 p.m."

I opened the letter, and this is what it contained:

"You will be surprised to see from my address that I am in London. I have had an operation for polypus in my nose. Miss Iseke is with me, and the operation has been quite successful. Please come and see me."

We summoned a cab and went off at once to the address given. We found Mother in a small lodging-house with Miss Iseke. The room was gloomy and looked dirty, and Mother none too comfortable. However, she seemed quite cheerful and pleased to see us. She said she had not told my Father about the operation as she thought it would worry him. She expected to go home on Saturday, all being well. It was then Tuesday.

Eleanor came round again the next day to see me and suggested I should look in the crystal again, which I did. I saw Mother in bed with her face and head bandaged, looking frightfully ill. Then I saw Eleanor come into the room, followed by a doctor and a nurse. I realised that Mother was very seriously ill.

We were worried about this, but we both agreed Mother had seemed all right when we saw her. However, we hurried round to see her and to reassure ourselves. Mother had been out in the morning, and we arranged that I should go to the Wallace Collection with her on the following day,

Thursday, which we did, and had a very pleasant time. I felt there was every prospect of Mother going home on Saturday, and I saw no reason why I should not carry out a previous arrangement to catch the early morning train to Scotland on Friday. Eleanor looked in to say goodbye, as she was going away on Friday for the week-end, to her country house.

On Saturday morning Eleanor got a telegram from Miss Iseke which said: "Mother dangerously ill. Come at once."

Eleanor rushed up to London, saw Mother and the doctor and arranged for a specialist and a nurse. She also sent for Father, who was terribly upset and was hurt that he had not been told anything of the operation.

Mother had erysipelas in the head and was dangerously ill. She had her head bandaged up just as I had seen in the crystal. She recovered slowly, but we thought the operation should never have been performed in such unsuitable conditions.

It was a mercy she did not die.

*   *   *

One blazing hot day, when it was really too hot to do anything, I had promised Eleanor that I would spend the afternoon with her, and so I had to keep my promise.

When I arrived she said:

"I am anxious for you to psychometrise a letter from Norman for me." Norman was her daughter-in-law. Then she quickly added:

"I want to know if they are going to move house, also if she is going to have another child."

I was really annoyed with her; she knew quite well that I particularly disliked knowing who a letter was from or to be asked to answer any particular question. I always maintained that I had to make my mind a blank so as to receive whatever came, and if I was told who the letter was from and asked to answer a lot of questions, it was confusing and made everything difficult.

However, I took the letter and stood in the middle of the room, as I disliked coming in contact with any furniture while psychometrising. The sun was shining in the room, and it was hot, but I preferred the daylight and would not have the curtains drawn.

I had hardly got the letter in my hand when I felt very ill. I became worse. I went very cold and could feel nothing in my arm and side. I said:

"There is a man who is very ill, paralysed down his left side. The condition is caused by injury to the spine; he is with relations who think he will recover, but he will die quite soon."

By this time my looks had frightened Eleanor and she took the letter out of my hands and rubbed my arm until I could feel it again. I sat quite quiet for a time, and then feeling much better, I said:

"Is there anything in the letter about illness?" and she said:

"No, it is about the grandchildren."

"Look again and see if you have missed anything."

She read the letter through and she had omitted to notice a P.S. on the back of the last sheet. It said:

"I have just heard from Mrs. B. that her son is ill."

Mrs. B's son was a friend of Eleanor's son who had died in the war, but Eleanor did not know him well.

No more was said at the time, but three days later, Eleanor had a letter from her daughter-in-law, saying:

"I have heard from Mrs. B. Her son is paralysed down the left side. It is caused by spine trouble, but he is getting on well and they have every hope of his recovery."

He was dead in a fortnight.

CHAPTER EIGHTEEN

FURTHER PSYCHIC EXPERIENCES

My cousin, Cornwallis Wykeham-Martin, once asked me to psychometrise one of the rooms at Leeds Castle. I assented readily and he chose for the experiment a room in the old Castle called Henry VIII's room. It was the room my parents always occupied when they stayed there. I went alone into the room, and had been there some time without any result. Then suddenly the room changed, it was no longer the comfortably furnished, rather modern room, but cold and bare, with little furniture and no carpet. There was a large fireplace, not in the situation of the present one, with logs burnings on the hearth. Then I saw a tall woman wearing a long flowing white robe, her hair hanging loose, pacing up and down the length of the room, wringing her hands and evidently in great distresss.

Cornwallis was interested. He told me that at one time Queen Joan of Navarre, stepmother of Henry V, had been imprisoned in that room for a few days on her way to Pevensey, and thence to France. And now I quote from my Grandfather's book:

"The Queen was accused of witchcraft and of trying by this means to kill her stepson, the King. She was despoiled of all her goods, beds, etc., and given a small allowance until shortly before Henry's death, when apparently his conscience smote him and he ordered all her moneys and goods to be restored to her. She came back to Leeds Castle and stayed there until she went to Havering-atte-Bower, where she lived till she died, 1437."

*   *   *

Eleanor took me to tea with her friend, Lady Thomson, who was interested in psychic matters and for this reason was anxious to make my acquaintance.

We had tea and after discussing psychic phenomena in a general way, Lady Thomson said, "I have just bought a cottage in Buckinghamshire. Can you tell me if it will be lucky for me?"

I said I did not see how I could possibly psychometrise the cottage without going to it, or at any rate having something tangible to hold. Then I asked, "Could you draw me a plan of the house?"

I knew she was an artist and I thought she might be able to do this. She was delighted and at once drew a plan of the downstairs rooms. There was a passage through the cottage from front to back, with a room on either side of the front door, and the kitchen and scullery at the back.

I was at once attracted to the room on the right of the front door, and said, "It is a small room and there is a large old-fashioned fireplace where logs are burning."

"No, that is not so," said Lady Thomson, "it is just an ordinary modern fireplace."

I, however, still visualised the fireplace, and then I saw a little girl, apparently very badly injured—I thought burned. She was carried by some people to the room on the other side of the front door, where she died almost immediately. I saw nothing else.

Lady Thomson was interested, and said she was going to the cottage in a day or two, and would try and find out something of its history for me.

About a week later she went down to the cottage, and when she arrived she found a great surprise awaiting her. The workmen had to replace some worn skirting boards near the fireplace in the room on the right of the front door. They had found after removing the skirting boards that there was a gap behind. They investigated and found the modern fireplace there had been built up in front of an old open fireplace like the one I had described.

This made Lady Thomson more keen than ever on finding out the history of the cottage. She asked many people, with no success, until someone suggested that an old man, who had lived all his life in the village, might remember something. Lady Thomson went at once to see him, and she told him how they had found the old fireplace, and asked him whether he knew anything about it.

"Oh, yes," he said at once, "there was an old open fireplace there many years ago, but there was a dreadful accident when a little girl was left alone in the room. She fell into the fire and was badly burned, and she died after they had moved her into the room on the other side of the passage. After this tragedy the old fireplace was built up, and a new modern grate put in."

*　　*　　*

My cousin Bertha, who had a property in South Africa which she visited every year, came to me on her return from one of her visits and brought with her a few stones and some earth from her farm. She asked me to try to find water on the estate. I took the stones and earth in my hand and shut my eyes. I then gave an exact description of the lie of the land, and said, "You have tried in a wrong quarter for the water." I then described the situation where the water was to be found.

Bertha sent instructions for this site to be explored, and sure enough the water was there.

*　　*　　*

I had a great friend called Cissie MacRae. We met when we were both quite young; she was an ardent member of the Suffragettes. Her mother lived in the dower house on the shores of Loch Fyne in Scotland. After her mother's death, her brother begged Cissie to keep on the dower house at Ballimore. This she did, and I stayed with her nearly every year. She took a flat every winter in London, and we did many things together. Her youngest brother,

The Author and her trough rock garden, 1961

The Author on her hundredth birthday, 1968

Sir Colin, was Lieutenant of the King's Bodyguard of the Yeoman of the Guard, and, through him, Cissie had tickets for many royal occasions to which she took me. On one occasion, it was a review of the Yeomen of the Guard in Buckingham Palace gardens—a very pretty sight. On another occasion, when he was on duty at Westminster Abbey at a distribution of the Maundy money, he gave us tickets for seats. It was quite easy, at the end of the ceremony, to meet some of the old pensioners outside, who, for a comparatively small sum, would part with their Maundy money. He also gave us tickets for a window in St. James's Palace overlooking the archway into St. James's Street on the occasion of the marriage of the Duke of Kent and Princess Marina. We had a wonderful view of the Duke and his lovely bride as they drove by in their carriage.

On Sundays we went to the beautiful old church of St. Ethelburga, situated in Bishopsgate, in the City. The parson was well known. His services were conducted on his own lines, and were entirely unlike the ordinary service. The choir was composed entirely of women, dressed in white, with long blue veils which hung down their backs. He was dressed like a monk. He was one of the few clergy-men who, in those days, consented to marry divorced people. I went there to one wedding of this description. He was also interested in psychic matters and there were many discussions on this subject at weekly meetings he had. We went to one, but unfortunately the time at which they were held made it impossible to go again.

Cissie was a wonderful friend and a great loss to me when she died. It was during one of my visits to her in Scotland that I had another psychic experience. Cissie came to me one morning with a letter. She said, "Alice, I think this will interest you very much. It is from some friends of mine who live the other side of the county. They have been very unfortunate in having to sell most of the estate, and only the house and a few acres of land now remain. The family consists of two sisters and a brother, middle-aged and with no near relations and no heir to the property. They possessed an old crystal which had been in the family for generations. This had suddenly and mysteriously disappeared, much to their concern. They had searched high and low and enquired amongst the crofters, and eventually given up all hope of finding it.

"In this letter they say the crystal has been recovered, and this is how it happened. There had been a heavy storm and some of the crofters had gone down to the foreshore in the morning to see whether anything of value had been washed up. One of them saw what he thought to be a piece of glass; he picked it up and examined it more closely and came to the conclusion that it was a crystal. Several people gathered round to look at his find, and one of them wondered whether it could be the crystal that the Laird set such store by and which had so mysteriously disappeared. It was certainly worth finding out. They took it up to the house, where it was acclaimed as the heirloom, much to the delight of the owners. They ask me whether I can persuade you to try and psychometrise it."

I had done much divination with Cissie at different times, and she had great faith in my powers and had told her friends about me. They were nervous of parting with their treasure even for a short time and sent it over by a special messenger on the understanding that they would send for it the next day. It was a curious-looking piece of crystal, about four inches in diameter, triangular in shape, rough and discoloured and cracked.

On holding it, I got the impression of some rather rough ground sloping down to the sea. There were no cliffs, only a bank, and on the bank I saw the ancient remains of a chapel. This I came to the conclusion had a great deal of history, but I could not get any further with it. I then described a man whom I saw ill in a hospital bed. Cissie at once exclaimed, "That is Ian" (the owner of the crystal). Several nurses were in attendance, and a priest who was obviously going to officiate. I knew that he was a

Roman Catholic. I also said, "The sick man is married. He will die quite soon." I got nothing further, and handed the crystal back to Cissie.

She said, "The only thing that you described rightly was the coastline and the old chapel which exists on the estate. The rest of it is absolutely untrue. He is certainly not a Roman Catholic; they are strict Presbyterians. Also he is not married, much to the disappointment of his sisters."

So that was that, and the crystal went back the following day. I heard no more until three months afterwards, when Cissie wrote me, "An extraordinary thing has happened. Everything you said about the Scotch crystal is true. The sisters had a telegram to say their brother was taken ill in Edinburgh and would they come at once. They found him in hospital and very ill, in fact there was little hope for his recovery. To their utter amazement, a Roman Catholic priest was at the bedside and administered the last rites. Their brother told them he had been a Roman Catholic for some time. He died the next day, and after his death it was disclosed that he had been secretly married for some time but there were no children."

*   *   *

Cissie introduced me to a friend of hers, Miss Milne, who was also very interested in psychic matters. One day when I was having tea with her she, knowing I sometimes used the powers I possessed, said:

"I wonder whether you could do anything for me."

I said I would try.

I used cards and told her I saw her packing up and that she would soon leave her flat. She asked why, and I said on account of a marriage, but not your own. She was living in a flat in London with a maid, Laura, who had been with her some years and of whom she was very fond. She said:

"I do not want to be rude, but it is quite impossible that I should be leaving my flat, I have no intention of doing so."

A few weeks later I heard through a mutual friend that

she was moving. Laura had settled rather hurriedly to marry, and, as Miss Milne did not want to part with her, she was moving into a larger flat so that she could accommodate the husband and give them a sitting-room. Some considerable time afterwards I met her again. She told me how right I had been and suggested I should tell her fortune again. She added:

"But please do not move me this time."

I used cards and I said:

"I am afraid I must move you again and that quite soon. This time you will go into the country to live." And I told her some details.

She was much astonished and said nothing was further from her thoughts than living in the country and also that Laura's husband had employment in London and was not likely to want to leave it. So we left it at that.

In two or three months' time she had bought a chicken farm in the country, I think with the idea of giving work to Laura's husband, who was proving rather unsatisfactory and had left his job in London. They moved and I went to see her in her new home. Once more we had recourse to the cards. This time I told her she would shortly go abroad, and that although she would intend to stay only a few weeks, she would, in fact, remain many months. She was perfectly happy where she was, she was very keen on the farm and hoping to turn it into a profitable concern and had no thought of going away, much less abroad. Within ten days she heard from a friend, who was on her way from Australia to transact some important business in Norway. For this she needed help and begged Miss Milne to go with her. As it was only to be for a few weeks Miss Milne agreed to accompany her.

The business turned out to be much more difficult and took much longer than expected. The few weeks were extended to nearly a year.

*   *   *

Cissie and I had many psychic experiences together and went to many seances, including some arranged by Conan Doyle. These we thought rather bogus. Conan Doyle was, I think, taken in, and the mediums he had at his seances did not strike us as being genuine. The seance was accompanied by prayers and hymns, and we were neither impressed nor convinced.

The following is a sample of the sort of procedure at many seances. The medium, standing on a platform, says: "I see an old lady, hair parted in the middle, very pleasant face, rather high cheekbones; she is smiling. She is dressed in a dark dress, and she has something on her dress. I am not sure whether it is a locket or a brooch. She passed over a few years ago. I hear her say, John and George and, I think, Arthur. Does anybody know who this is?"

In a large crowd, it is almost certain that someone will claim this person as their mother.

Then the medium will start again, saying something like this: "I see a young man in uniform, khaki uniform, he is very young and fair. He wants to give a message to Mary. He wants her to be happy. He has not forgotten her, and he is often with her."

I never found this sort of thing convincing, though I have to admit that I was impressed by what I heard about the famous psychic Denis Bradley, who used to hold wonderful seances at his Wimbledon house. He had written several books on the subject. In one of them was a description of a seance at which the Countess of Arnheim was present and the medium told her most wonderful things. I believe this medium was not a highly cultured person and had no knowledge of languages. The Countess was Russian, and the medium spoke to her in Russian, giving her information concerning her brother to whom she was devoted. He mentioned intimate matters concerning their early life, which no one else could possibly have known.

I knew the Countess of Arnheim, and she told me that

the medium also spoke in Chinese to the Chinese Ambassador, at the same seance.

I was keen to meet Mr. Bradley, and the Countess duly introduced me to him. We talked for some time chiefly about psychic matters, but I did not feel at ease with him and had a strange feeling that he was slightly antagonistic to me. However, he asked me to come down to his house, and we settled a date. Eleanor was with me, and she was included in the invitation.

When Eleanor and I arrived at the Bradleys, we had rather a cool reception from Mrs. Bradley and she informed us that Mr. Bradley was away. This was a disappointment, as he had invited us, and I was confirmed in my suspicion that he was antagonistic to me.

After a while two other ladies, one of whom, Mrs. Cory, was a friend of Eleanor's, turned up. Mrs. Cory at once began to suggest our going to the seance room and trying some experiments. Mrs. Bradley was reluctant and made excuses, one of which was that her son was probably having tea there. We then had tea, and Mrs. Cory again suggested a seance. Eventually it was arranged that I should go alone to the seance room and see if I got any impressions. I went into the room and stood still for a few minutes, when I began to have a curious sensation of levitation. I could not keep on my feet and had to stand on tip-toe with a feeling I might go up. I did not like it much and went back to the drawing-room.

By this time Mrs. Cory had arranged we should go to the seance room and try to get the direct voice. This I had never experienced. We all went into the room and Mrs. Cory and I moved an old coffin-stool into the middle of the room and Mrs. Bradley produced a trumpet which was placed on it. It was rather like a hunting-horn. We all stood round it. At first nothing happened, then suddenly the trumpet began moving about rapidly, then stopped and we all heard distinctly the roll of a drum.

Eleanor's eldest son, who was in France with his regiment, played the drum well, and she thought it had some message for her; but nothing else happened, no direct voice, much to my disappointment. We then put our hands on the stool, allowing our fingers to touch, and after a second or two the stool, which was heavy, rose gradually, while we retained our fingers on it. It rose so high I had to reach up to keep my hands on it. It then gradually descended. This happened three times, and then nothing else. No one was attempting any trickery; in fact it would have been quite impossible to move the stool even if we had all pressed hard.

I never saw any more of the Bradleys.

I have never had any experience of what is called the direct voice. The nearest approach I have had to it was when my friend Janet asked me to help her. Janet was an unhappy woman and spent a lot of time consulting mediums and attending seances, which I think was a great mistake. She went to some mediums who were obviously getting money out of her. One day she said, "I wish you would try and get something for me."

I was sorry for her and felt I must try to do anything I could to help her. I therefore put myself into a receptive state. I stood in the middle of the room, and let my mind become blank. In this state I felt nothing and saw nothing and words flowed from me for at least half an hour. At the end of this I did not know what I had said, but she was enthralled.

I did this again frequently during the next few weeks and apparently it helped her a great deal. She had lost her faith in her religion but she was not really an atheist. The communication she received through me helped her to solve her doubts and difficulties, which made her life much happier.

That was the only time I was used in that sort of way.

I have sometimes given warnings. My brother Robert had a business which he had worked up through many setbacks and difficulties, and was just beginning to reap the results of his labours when the First World War broke out. He joined up, and before he went abroad, he consulted me. I told him that his manager—a man who had been years with him and whom he trusted implicitly—was untrustworthy, and I foresaw that he would do harm to the business in Robert's absence.

Robert was annoyed at this suggestion and scoffed at the idea. He left the business almost entirely in the manager's hands. The result was that the manager, having first of all abused Robert to the clients and installed himself in their good books, left the business and set up for himself and took the majority of the best clients with him. Robert's wife was terribly upset but could do little, and by the time Robert got back from the war the business was in a sorry state. He never got it back to the flourishing state it had been in when he left for the war. There were one or two law-suits, and Robert gained them all, but without any real benefit, as the former clients had believed the stories which had been told and did not return to him.

I have never been successful with tea-cups; for some unknown reason they convey absolutely nothing to me. I have often seen it done with good results, and at one time there was a professional woman I used to go and consult, and of all the different professionals I have met I think she was the most successful with me.

Photographs sometimes convey a great deal to me, and I am almost always able to tell if the person is alive or dead. Handwriting is also a means of getting many facts of a person's life, but again, when it comes to more than mere character, I think you need clairvoyance.

I have sometimes been quite successful with palmistry, although I am not at all expert. At one time I studied several books on the subject but never made much progress with it, and in fact the results I did get were, I am sure, due to clairvoyance and not to the accepted reading of the lines. I am sure that anyone able to read a hand must be gifted with clairvoyance, possibly without being aware of the fact.

The planchette is another means used to dip into the

past and to attempt to foretell future events. It is a heart-shaped board on wheels, with a hole for a pencil. It is placed on a large blank sheet of paper. Two people then put the tips of their fingers on it, and either they or some other person ask questions. The board then moves backwards and forwards, enabling the pencil to write answers to the questions.

I have often seen this done and have myself been one of the persons to put fingers on the board. As far as I am concerned it has never been a success. I have come to the conclusion that there is a good deal of self-hypnotism about it, for I have been conscious on many occasions that the other person working with me is pushing the board to say what they wish. I do not think they are always aware that they are doing this, and would be angry if you suggested they were doing so.

I have known people who have told me they never do anything of importance without consulting the board. People always ask who is guiding the pencil and they are generally told it is a relation who is dead. I am told that often it is a priest, and in one case where people constantly consulted the board they said a priest controlled it and that sometimes he was drunk, and that when this was so he was very blasphemous.

I did it with a man at one time and he always hurriedly asked who was controlling it: the answer was always the same—his "Aunt Bessie". Then he immediately began asking questions about how certain money and estates were going to be left and many things to do with his own affairs. I found by watching his hands and the muscles of his wrists that he was undoubtedly using force himself. I several times let my fingers weigh heavily enough on the board to prevent this, and he got very angry and said I was no medium and he could get nothing when I helped. I do not think he was in the least aware of what he was doing.

This, I think, shows the danger of the whole performance. On the other hand, there are instances of things of importance being divulged, as, for instance, the well-known case of Bligh Bond and Glastonbury Abbey. He used a pencil only—automatic writing. This is done by holding the pencil between your first and third finger, the pencil resting on the second finger. You then have a sheet of paper and let the pencil have its will.

Bligh Bond said a monk controlled the pencil and gave him accurate details of where the foundation of the Loretto Chapel in Glastonbury Abbey could be found. The authorities allowed digging to take place, and the foundations of the Chapel were found. There was a great deal of talk about it at the time and, I think, some unpleasantness. Bligh Bond wrote a very interesting book called *The Gate of Remembrance*, explaining all that happened. I met him on several occasions and heard him lecture.

It was claimed that, although it was known that the Loretto Chapel had existed, no one knew the site. I was told that this was not so, and that the Roman Catholics had plans of the Chapel in their keeping. If this was so, of course one cannot rule out the possibility of telepathy as a medium, and it is possible Bligh Bond's mind was working —of course unconsciously—all the time.

CHAPTER NINETEEN

THE ISLE OF WIGHT MYSTERY

IT was in the year 1921 that Hugh and I had an invitation to stay with our friends, the Scotts, who lived near Ventnor in the Isle of Wight.

Mr. Scott and Hugh went one morning into Ventnor to have their hair cut. The barber shop is, I think, the man's place for gossip. When they arrived back, they told us there was great excitement over a skeleton which had been found in the garden of Craigie Lodge, a house quite close to the Scotts. It was reported that a skeleton of a child had been dug up when a tree was being planted in the bank. The doctor had come and taken the bones away and he had consulted another doctor about them. They both pronounced them to be of fairly recent burial, that is to say certainly under twenty years.

During lunch the Scotts told us what they had heard of the history of Craigie Lodge. It had previously been owned by Mrs. Craigie (the authoress who wrote under the name of John Oliver Hobbes). Mrs. Craigie was separated from her husband; she could not divorce him as she was a Roman Catholic.

She was very friendly with a German family called Spiller. Mr. Spiller was the head of a big firm of dyers in Germany. He had bought a large house about a mile away, ostensibly for holidays, and came there frequently.

He had employed German workmen on his estate, and the Scotts had been told that they had made a concrete landing-place where his estate sloped down to the shore.

Mr. Spiller had said that this was to be for the benefit of the local fishermen, although they did not appear to need it. The Islanders did not like him and were very suspicious of his activities.

His workmen were also employed to lay out the garden of Craigie Lodge. Just before war was declared in 1914, he hastily left the Island and never returned. The house had been left empty and was going to rack and ruin. His son, who was an artist of some repute, and had exhibited his paintings in Paris, stayed behind, taking a small house next door to Craigie Lodge, where his father's old butler and wife looked after him.

The young Mr. Spiller and Mrs. Craigie became great friends and were constantly seen together. The story got about that they had been overheard to have a violent quarrel one day when walking in the garden, after which she went straight up to her flat in London and the next day was found dead from an overdose of sleeping tablets. At the inquest the verdict was accidental death. Young Spiller immediately left his house and did not return.

We were interested, and after lunch I asked Dorothy Scott if we could walk down the road and see what we could see. The garden of Craigie Lodge, which was large and very lovely, was separated from the house by a lane. We had just reached the garden when two ladies came out of Craigie Lodge.

"Here are Mrs. and Miss Capell," said Dorothy, and was going to say "how do you do" and introduce me when Mrs. Capell said, "Good gracious, it is Alice Wykeham-Martin!"

I immediately recognised her as Marie Capell, the girl who became engaged the same day as I did. I had entirely lost touch with her, but I did know that Marie's marriage had been a failure. I now heard that she had divorced her husband and had reverted to her maiden name, calling herself Mrs. Capell.

They were delighted to meet me again, and Marie said, "A skeleton has just been found in our garden. I remember what a witch you were. Do come and see if you can find out anything."

We proceeded into the garden and I was shown the place from which the skeleton had been removed. It had not been more than two feet below the surface. I put my hand down on to the grave and immediately said, "There is another skeleton here."

They were terrifically excited and asked me to try and locate the exact spot.

"If you take a trowel and dig carefully about," I said, "you will come across some bones of the first skeleton, and if you can get these I may be able to tell you more."

Dorothy and I went home; that was on Friday. On Saturday morning Dora Capell arrived and said they had found something—"bits of bone close to the grave". She suggested that I should go and try to psychometrise again. I arranged to go round on Sunday afternoon. They had two bones in a little silver box, and I tipped them out into my hand.

I at once said, "I can tell you where the other skeleton is. If you dig about a foot from where the head of the child's skeleton was, you will find the skeleton of a woman, lying North to South."

The next morning Hugh and I went back to London. Hugh was going out for the evening and I thought it a good opportunity to go and dine with Eleanor. In the middle of dinner the parlourmaid came to say I was wanted on the telephone. It was Alison who said, "A man from *The Times* wanted to speak to you."

"There must be a mistake," I said. "There are several Pollocks associated with newspapers. He probably wanted one of them."

"No, it was you," said Alison, "and it was about a skeleton which has been found in the Isle of Wight."

It appeared that the Capells had dug where I told them and had discovered the other skeleton, a woman lying in the position I had indicated. They had communicated with the Police about this skeleton and they had removed it. The press got hold of the story and it was on the placards in London: "Barrister's wife finds skeleton in the Isle of Wight."

In the meantime the matter had been reported to the coroner and the question arose as to whether there should be an inquest or not. The coroner had consulted a man who was an authority on such matters, and he had declared the bones to be of ancient origin. This being so there would not have to be an inquest. However, owing to all the talk, the coroner eventually decided to have an inquest.

This he did, and I stayed with the Scotts again in order to be present at it. Neither the gardener nor Marie Capell was called. Very little evidence was given, and the coroner accepted the verdict that the bones were prehistoric. He mentioned that he and his colleagues had been to see the place where the skelton had been found and, much to our surprise, said that the ground was rough and stony. We were quite aware that this was not the case.

Marie Capell had expressed a wish to have the bones of the skeleton to give them Christian burial, and this the coroner agreed to. After the inquest we all, including the gardener, went back to the burial place and Marie told the gardener to dig down to the bottom of the bank to show that the soil was comparatively soft and easily removed. In the evening, a sack, containing what was said to be the remains of the two skeletons, arrived at Marie Capell's. She had arranged with a clergyman friend of hers to have them buried in his churchyard. The next morning, early, a messenger arrived to say that the bones were not to be left with her as they were of great historic interest. The final report was as follows:

"These remains have a medico-legal value, and it is desirable that they should not be destroyed by burial, but preserved in the medico-legal collection at the Royal College of Surgeons." This ended the matter.

I had an amusing time in London with the press, who

came in large numbers to my house. Also I received a great
number of letters, many from abroad, some of them very
pathetic. I was requested to find anything from a lost
kitten, a piece of whose bedding was enclosed, to a missing
husband. I had a letter from Prince Louis de Bourbon,
which was as follows:

"LE CRIBLE"
Revue-Journal
PARIS, 39, Rue Caumartin, (9e)

                                        le 29 octobre 1921
Madame,
            Les journaux français ayant reconté les merveil-
leuses facultés que vous possèdez et l'usage altruiste que
vous en faites, j'ai pensé que vous voudriez peut-être faire
usage de ces facultés au profit d'une personne qui vient de
faire une perte très cruelle. Une dame, appartenant à la
meilleure société, a laissé, lors d'un récent retour de voyage,
dans un taxi-auto, une petite mallette contenant ses bijoux
de famille (heirlooms).
    La valeur de ces bijoux dépasse un million de francs,
mais la perte lui en est surtout très cruelle à cause des
souvenirs qui s'y attachent. Si vous voulez entendre l'appel
que je vous addresse, j'aurais l'honneur de vous mettre en
rapport avec la personne dont les bijoux ont été perdue.
    Avec mes remerciements anticipés, je vous prie d'agréer,
Madame, les assurances de ma Très Haute considération,

                                Louis, Prince de Bourbon.

I did not consent to unravel the mystery of the jewels,
neither did I do more than acknowledge the many letters I
got, by a formal note saying I was not a professional.
    I had several anonymous letters suggesting that there
had been foul play and urging me to continue investigations.
This was quite impossible, as the Capells were using the
Ouija board, the press were busy, and the whole atmosphere
became unsuitable.

There was a good deal of mystery attached to the whole matter. For one thing the butler was seen by the Capells to go out with a lantern and search about by the grave, two nights running. He said to Mrs. Capell, "They aren't old bones. I know they come from the Carfax." The Carfax was a public house a short way up the road. Another odd thing he and his wife did was to bring large bundles of things, chiefly clothes and papers, from the house and burn them on bonfires. They had two or three of these bonfires. They had charge of a child living in their house. This child used to creep through the hedge into the Capells' garden, and they were very kind to him. They found he was mentally retarded and responded to their kindness with pathetic affection.

I never visited the Isle of Wight again.

Some months later I had an anonymous letter about the mystery, saying that Mr. Spiller was living in a London hotel, and was drugging himself to death. The writer enclosed a table napkin that Mr. Spiller had used, and asked me to psychometrise it, which I did not do—and as the article was of small value I burned it. This was the last I heard of the whole affair.

CHAPTER TWENTY

MY CONCLUSIONS ON THE SUPERNATURAL

My psychic experiences have convinced me that there is a psychic sense lying dormant in all human beings. At certain times this sense shows itself, sometimes only momentarily, enabling future events to be foreseen or past ones described. This sense cannot be forced, it comes and goes unbidden, but there is no doubt that by putting oneself into a receptive state of mind one is able to receive information.

The things I tell come to me—how or why I do not know—they come and I simply tell them. I am not in trance, but sometimes I do not realise what I am saying. As the psychic sense became more obvious, I was persuaded to try to use it for people anxious about their future. For this purpose I tried the usual methods of fortune telling—which I found only helped me to reach a state where all ordinary senses were in abeyance. The crystal or cards really conveyed nothing, but concentration on them helped me to make my mind a blank ready to receive psychic impressions. I found that almost immediately I became aware of a vision of places and actions apart from my normal consciousness. These visions either portrayed past events, or predicted future events. The past was in many cases verified after I had described it. The future was almost always fulfilled, sometimes several months later.

Under these conditions I have got some astounding results, giving information which sometimes had no apparent connection with the person enquiring.

People often ask questions about certain people and events; I never pretend I can answer them. I only get what comes to me and over this I have no control. I tell them just what comes and never try to get special information on any subject. If you try to get a particular thing for a person, your own imagination comes in. You must keep your mind a blank to receive what will come. This is where the professionals so often fail.

Prophecy and the interpretation of prophecies have been practised all through the ages. The wish to look into the future has been very persistent, and this has led to prophets or people with the psychic sense being treated with respect and veneration, and to their being raised to positions of importance, but their desire to obtain power and wealth led some of them to make wrong use of the psychic sense which, as I have already said, cannot be controlled.

As time went on and prophecies were seldom fulfilled, the whole practice fell into disrepute. Prophets were no longer held in high esteem, and fortune telling and witch-craft, as it came to be called, was looked upon with dis-approval and even punished by burning at the stake.

In spite of severe penalties, curiosity as to the future was not diminished and fortune-tellers continue to exist down to the present day.

I do not for one moment say that the professional fortune teller is entirely without some clairvoyante or psychic sense, but this sense is greatly diminished or lost when it is used for commercial gain.

The professional procedure is normally as follows. A room is set aside for the reception of clients and regular hours are kept for sittings. The room is dimly lit. In the middle of the room there are two chairs on opposite sides of a small table. Sometimes cards are used, but more often a crystal ball, on a piece of black velvet. One of the usual preliminaries is for the fortune teller to recount the marvellous things she has foretold, whetting the client's interest.

If cards are used they are shuffled by the client, and then laid out by the fortune teller. If she uses the crystal the client is requested to hold it for a few moments, and then the fortune teller looks into it, and the telling begins. She will probably ask the client whether there is any special question she would like to ask. The client is usually very eager to get down to business, and begins by saying:

"I don't want my character or past. What I really want to know is:

"Am I going to move house?" or

"Is my daughter going to marry?" or

"Is my husband going to leave me?"

All this gives the fortune teller the chance to foretell probabilities and the client goes away telling her friends of the wonderful woman she has been to, and quite unconscious of the fact that most of it has come from herself!

Although the fortune teller may occasionally be genuinely clairvoyant, she has no control over the psychic sense and more often than not she will be unreceptive, and there will certainly be people for whom she can see nothing. On these occasions if she is honest she will return the fee and say:

"I can do nothing for you today."

But then the client will be annoyed and will go away saying that the fortune teller is no good. This will be harmful for business, because the professional fortune teller depends entirely on personal recommendation.

I do not think professional mediums should be employed for research, which should only be conducted with mediums who have no desire for material gain. I think a wrong approach has often been made in this respect.

For example, one of the experiments to prove the existence of telepathy is as follows:

Two people are placed in separate rooms, with cards laid out for one of them, and this one has to try by telepathy to communicate the position and picture of the cards to the person in the other room. I do not think this is in any way satisfactory. It is too material an approach.

I am a firm believer in telepathy, and I think some people are able to communicate with one another when a long distance apart, but this gift should be used for conveying real thoughts and not for transmitting useless information. I think that this misuse is why this sort of scientific experiment is often a failure.

Some predictions are given as warnings. It is strange that in spite of all the curiosity about the future, inquirers often do not rely on the prediction sufficiently to act on the advice given.

One sees this with the old prophecies. They were so often disregarded with disastrous results.

Is it desirable to try to develop the psychic sense or not? What does it mean? A person gifted with this sense is enabled to see the past and the future, but they must accept what comes. We get sufficient to show us that there is this sense which we are allowed to use but not to develop fully. I see no reason why we should not use the sense as given to us but it should be used with care and certainly not commercially. If it were to be developed to any great extent what would it mean to life? To have complete knowledge of the future is to us quite incomprehensible. We must cast off the material of this world, and enter another before full revelation. Until that time my advice is, never let go of your courage, never give up hope.

I am content to wait.

PART THREE

I Enter My Second Century

CHAPTER TWENTY-ONE

THE SUN IS STILL SHINING

In 1921, when Hugh retired, we bought a house in Somerset called "Crossways". I was looking forward to village life as I remembered it, but I found, alas, a different sort of life. The village contained two factories, one a sawmill and the other a lace factory. The owner of the latter was a Nottingham man and he had brought workers from Nottingham who had settled in the village. I found it difficult to understand them as they were not my idea of real country people.

I did what I could to join the village activities and became President of the Women's Institute. There were so many different cliques (or, as our gardener used to say, "clicks") in the village, that it was very difficult to get them to work together. This "clickiness" annoyed me and I thought I would try and put an end to it. There were certain people who did the teas as a matter of course and it struck me that it would be a good thing to alter this and that the task should be allocated to different people every month. I therefore had all the names of the members written on separate bits of paper and, having told them what I intended to do, I called a woman forward to draw four names at a time. Each group of four were to do the teas for one month. This resulted in people being drawn together who were practically not on speaking terms! There was no open rebellion, though I do not think it was at all a popular move and I am not sure that it attained its objective. However, I had done my best. We had magic lantern shows and lectures and demonstrations of various sorts. One thing which always surprised me was their extraordinary delight in musical chairs, which they insisted on having at every meeting. It really was a funny sight to see these elderly women running round.

I also started a Natural History Society for the school children. I had heard of such cruel practices amongst the children. For instance, one amusement was to take un-fledged birds from the nest, put them on the road and throw stones at them till they were dead. The children became very keen, making maps of the fields, showing the places where the nests were, and writing essays. I had quite a large library of Natural History books for which they paid one penny when they took a book out to read. These pennies we used, when enough were accumulated, to buy more books. I sometimes wondered how lasting an interest this would be for the children and I was pleased when a boy came back to the village, after being employed at Sainsbury's in London for some years, and told me that he was so grateful to me for having given him an interest which would last him all his life.

When we first went to Crossways the garden was in a deplorable state. The house had originally been two cottages which had been converted into a residence for some people whose only interest was in horses and hunting. There were about two acres of land, consisting of the old cottage gardens close to the house and the rest was a paddock. Hugh and the gardener made a large kitchen garden out of part of the paddock. The improvement of the cottage garden round the house I superintended myself. I had a good tennis court made and to celebrate our silver wedding I planted yew trees between that and the kitchen garden and down one side of the kitchen garden, making a long grass path between it and our boundary hedge, with a seat at the far end. On the boundary side of this path I planted laburnum trees.

Nearer to the house and opposite the drawing-room

window I had a wide grass path with a broad herbaceous border on each side of it. Beyond the herbaceous borders I made a rock garden. There had been an old wall right across the garden and pulling this down gave me the stones I needed. I had a crazy paving path from the verandah to the kitchen garden with anemones on either side of it. These did remarkably well and I have never seen finer anemones.

The greatest compliment I was ever paid about my garden was from Helen Granville-Barker, who said when she was leaving a party at our house:

"I have never seen a garden that I have liked better than yours. It looks as though every flower in it is loved."

I think Crossways was haunted. Our gardener's wife, who had been housemaid to our predecessors, told me that she saw her former mistress (who had been dead several years) looking out of the window as she approached the house. Also in the best spareroom, Eleanor, who stayed with me several times, said she was certain there was some "presence" in the room. She also had an extraordinary feeling about a wardrobe in that room.

We rented a nice stretch of trout fishing on the Axe. Amongst our many visitors who enjoyed this fishing was James Wentworth Day, now so well known for his books on sport. It is amusing to think that he caught his first trout when staying with us. On a former occasion, when he stayed with us at Bunessan, on the Isle of Mull, where we had rented a shooting (woodcock and snipe) I only knew him very slightly. We just managed to get enough woodcock to have one each for dinner the night he arrived. Much to my surprise, when the woodcock were put on the table, he turned almost green in the face and we discovered that the sight and smell of the woodcock, instead of being the pleasant surprise that I expected, made him almost faint. A plate of cold ham was produced for him and Hugh and I shared the spare woodcock.

After dinner the conversation turned on psychic subjects

and Mr. Wentworth Day said that he had heard that I was clairvoyante. He asked me whether I could tell him anything and would I look at his hand. I said I really did not do palmistry, but I would see what I could do. I held his hand and told him several things that interested him. Then I said "If I did not know that it was not so, I should say that you were married." There was a pause—then he gasped out:

"But I am married. I was married at a registrar's office in London just before I came up here."

I think this points to telepathy, as no doubt his mind would have been preoccupied with thoughts of his bride.

The next day I must report that he shot his first snipe with us, but he did not have it for dinner!

We also tried on several occasions to get rough shooting near Crossways, but every time we found that poaching made it worthless. On one farm we had rented the farmer and his son went out early in the morning when they knew that we were coming that day and shot everything they could find. On another shoot we went out at 6 a.m., hoping to catch somebody in the act. We surprised the owner of the village shop just about to loose off at a sitting pheasant. He saw us and ran for his life. We gave up that shoot and afterwards contented ourselves with the fishing.

After twelve years we decided to return to London, as the garden was too much for me and Hugh, who had been a good carpenter, found it was now too strenuous for him. He had made a wonderful front door for Crossways of solid oak with iron hinges and many other useful articles. We took a flat and soon found pleasure in meeting some of our old London friends again.

Hugh died within a few months of the end of the Second World War, after which I lived alone for seven years. When Alison became a widow, in 1951, I went to live with her in Somerset where, once again, I was able to take an interest in village life. I joined the Women's Institute and entered for all sorts of competitions such as toymaking, crochet and floral decoration and won several prizes. I received first prize at a flower show for a miniature garden which I made in a baking dish. I took a lot of pains with it. For the grass lawn I sowed the seeds and cut the grass with nail scissors, making a really nice lawn which ran down to a pond, represented by a looking-glass in a hollow, with a willow tree hanging over it. The whole thing was surrounded by a hedge and many flowers.

One of the toys I made was a dolls' house complete with furniture. I made this out of a wooden box in which I put partitions, making two rooms upstairs and a kitchen and sitting-room downstairs. I papered the walls, cut out windows and put up curtains. I made a staircase, which ascended from the kitchen, and even put in a splendid lavatory! The bedroom had a fourposter bed and a cot for the baby. There were small dolls to represent the family. The father was dressed in a sporting suit and the mother was very smartly dressed. There was also a nurse in uniform. I bought a toy stove, saucepans and frying pan for the kitchen. I thatched the roof with straw and made a small garden in front. It created quite a sensation at the show, where it received a second prize. Eventually I gave this dolls' house to a little girl who had broken her leg and she had endless enjoyment from it.

In 1957 we moved to Haslemere. I was still very interested in gardening, but unable to do anything which entailed stooping. When on one occasion I returned from a visit to David, I found that Alison had had a brick trough built for me. It was 3 ft. 6 in. high, 6 ft. long and 3 ft. wide, with drainage holes at the bottom and filled up with good soil. There were also stones with which I made a miniature rock garden. It is difficult to describe the intense pleasure that this has given me—once again to have a rock garden to tend and enjoy. I have a variety of tiny trees and plants and there is some colour in it nearly every month of the year. One of my greatest joys is my miniature lilac bush which produces a mass of blossom in the spring.

I have always led a busy life and like to feel that I can still be useful, so I occupy my time by making shawls for bed-ridden women. I collect wool from all my friends and, by mixing the colours, I can make them bright and gay. I make not less than one a month and when I have got half a dozen finished I send them to places as far apart as Devon, Tibet, Glasgow, Austria and Edinburgh as well as distributing a few locally.

I have so much to be grateful for, and I am glad to feel that I can be of service to those who are less fortunate than I am. I do not feel old in myself—it is only when I move that I realise my age.

My memory takes me back over a hundred and two years of a happy life. There have been some dark clouds but they have drifted past to reveal a sun still shining in the sky.

APPENDIX I

Letter from Captain Nelson to

> Honourable William Cornwallis
> No. 4 Corke Street,
> London.
>   Burnham
>   Oct. 13th 1788

My dear Friend,

I received your kind letter on Saturday, and was sorry to think that you could suppose any situation in life could ever diminish the ardour, I trust it has been always conspicuous, I have to serve my country (although I am as happy in domestic life as any person can be). My wish has been (for I may now say a series of years) to serve under you. However, I trust you have selected Officers who will do credit to your choice, more able ones I am sensible are easily met with but one more attached or affectionate than myself I will not so readily yield to. Such things has been that Officers have not liked to go to India, although I have no doubt but your penetration is too good to have made a choice where such a thing could happen.

But should any event take place which should increase the number of ships, or prevent any of your present choice from going and none presenting themselves who you will wisely prefer to your rural friend, always recollect that I can leave my humble and peaceful cottage and believe me as ever your faithful and affectionate,

>   Horatio Nelson

Pardon my sending the enclosed. If it is of any use it will give me satisfaction.

The Enclosure.

Our Master in the Seahorse was a very clever man, and we constantly took the Lunar Observations; therefore I have no doubt but you will find the Seahorse's Log book almost (if not the best) of any in the Navy Office. It would be impertinent of me to say much on this subject. We went the outward passage, made the Islands of St. Paul and Amsterdam before we haul'd to the Northward. The only caution in approaching the peninsular of India is to be assured you are well to the Eastward, for in April, May and June the currents often set so strong to the Westward that ships fancying themselves far to the Eastward and to the Northward of Ceylon, haul up Westerly and get foul of the Maldives, or are so far up the Malabar Coast that great risk is run in getting round Ceylon again. There is no danger whatever in keeping well to the Eastward, and with the S.W. Monsoon, which then blows—when half way up the Island of Ceylon 100 or 150 Lgs. is very soon run, with the wind a point free or clean full.

*   *   *

Letter from Admiral Lord Nelson & Brontë to

> Honourable William Cornwallis.
> Victory off Cape St. Marys
> May 27th 1805

My dear Friend,
        The enemy's fleet from the West Indies being certainly gone to some port in the Bay, I am proceeding to the Northward with Eleven sail of the Line. I shall either call off Cape Clear, or proceed direct off Ushant to form a Junction with you as circumstances may in my Judgement (from Intelligence) require. I shall only hope after all my long pursuit of my enemy that I may arrive at the moment they are meeting you, for my very wretched state of health will force me to get on shore for a little while. I am ever my dear Friend your most faithful and attached.

Nelson and Brontë

APPENDIX II

Letter from Fiennes Wykeham Martin to his Stepmother.

Camp near Balaclava
October 27th, 1854.

Dear Mama,

I write you a line to allay any fears you may have about me, as you will see by *The Times* that the Light Cavalry Brigade were let into a sort of Chillianwallah trap and cut to pieces. It is unfortunately too true; but I am one of the lucky ones that escaped, although our regiment and the 11th Hussars went further than any into the gorge. The facts of the case are these. Lately the Cavalry have had nothing to do but guard Balaklava, and keep the communication open between it and Sevastopol, and have not been disturbed by the enemy except in occasional skirmishes with the pickets and videttes, when suddenly the other morning at day-break they made an attack on a line of small forts kept by the Turks in front of our position. The Cavalry, who were all out and mounted for the usual morning parade, that we always have an hour or two before daybreak, so as to be ready for any attack, went immediately to their support, with a troop of Horse Artillery; but could you believe it, the Turks left all the forts, some even before they were fired; the consequence was a swarm of Cavalry made a dash into Balaklava itself, but they were met on the left by the 93rd Highlanders, who are not in the habit of running away like the Turks, and sent back minus a few men, and on the right by the Heavy Cavalry, who likewise sent them to the right about, the Light Brigade being too far to the left to be able to pursue. This was a mistake, and now comes the melancholy part of my story. The Light Brigade were ordered to the front, and Nolan, "my friend", brought an order for us to attack them down a long valley they had retreated into; now to understand why we did this rash and stupid act, you must know that lately there has been some stupid chaff about the Cavalry being afraid of the

Cossacks, and Nolan had made some remarks about it to Lord Lucan, he is *rather suspected*, as he was the man sent to make the reconnaissance before we attacked, of having misrepresented to Lord Raglan the nature of the ground and the position of the enemy. Well, the Light Brigade advanced at a trot, and had not gone ahundred yards before we got into a shower of grape shot bullets, round shot, and in fact every kind of missile from both sides of the valley, the enemy having got a battery on each side, and two or three regiments of sharp-shooters in bushes. The consequence was we were enfiladed for half a mile by the hottest possible fire at about 30 or 40 yards distance, nevertheless we passed on, got beyond their fire, and captured some guns and drove back their Cavalry. But by this time we found ourselves completely cut off from our own army, about 90 of the Brigade left with a swarm of Cavalry in our front, a regiment of Russian Lancers in our rear, and all the fire to undergo again. Well the only thing to do was to get the debris together, and go at them with all our might and cut our way back, which some of us succeeded in doing, but when we got back and came to count heads, we found there were only 190 left out of 700 that went into action. Poor Halkett and Sparke are among the missing; Hutton was shot through both legs and in the back, but will recover I think. We are now a perfect skeleton of a regiment, only having 50 left, and are therefore useless. We live in the hope of being sent home to recruit up again, and being sent out again in the spring, but I am afraid they will hardly do that. Poor Nolan was shot the first ball.